50 Cooking for Fitness Recipes for Home

By: Kelly Johnson

Table of Contents

- Grilled Chicken Breast with Steamed Broccoli
- Baked Salmon with Asparagus
- Turkey and Quinoa Stuffed Bell Peppers
- Spicy Tofu Stir-Fry with Brown Rice
- Egg White Omelette with Spinach and Mushrooms
- Greek Yogurt Parfait with Fresh Berries and Granola
- Quinoa and Black Bean Salad with Avocado
- Lean Beef Stir-Fry with Mixed Vegetables
- Oven-Roasted Turkey Breast with Sweet Potatoes
- Shrimp and Vegetable Skewers with Quinoa
- Chicken and Vegetable Curry with Brown Rice
- Veggie-Packed Turkey Chili
- Baked Cod with Lemon and Herbs
- Tofu and Vegetable Stir-Fry with Quinoa
- Grilled Steak Salad with Balsamic Vinaigrette
- Seared Tuna Nicoise Salad
- Baked Chicken Thighs with Roasted Brussels Sprouts
- Lentil and Vegetable Soup
- Teriyaki Salmon with Stir-Fried Vegetables
- Quinoa and Vegetable Stuffed Bell Peppers
- Turkey Meatballs with Zucchini Noodles
- Baked Sweet Potato Fries with Greek Yogurt Dip
- Chicken Caesar Salad with Whole Grain Croutons
- Vegetarian Lentil Sloppy Joes
- Grilled Veggie and Chicken Skewers
- Spaghetti Squash with Turkey Bolognese Sauce
- Turkey and Spinach Meatloaf
- Greek Yogurt Chicken Salad Wraps
- Tuna Salad Stuffed Avocados
- Quinoa and Black Bean Stuffed Zucchini Boats
- Egg White Breakfast Burritos with Salsa
- Turkey and Vegetable Lettuce Wraps
- Baked Chicken Tenders with Honey Mustard Dip
- Veggie and Egg Scramble
- Seared Salmon with Roasted Vegetables

- Greek Yogurt Chicken Parmesan
- Shrimp and Avocado Lettuce Wraps
- Turkey and Sweet Potato Hash
- Grilled Vegetable Quinoa Bowl
- Baked Chicken Drumsticks with Roasted Cauliflower
- Mediterranean Chickpea Salad with Feta
- Egg White Breakfast Muffins with Spinach and Feta
- Turkey and Vegetable Kabobs with Quinoa
- Baked Cod with Tomato and Olive Relish
- Chicken and Quinoa Power Bowl
- Turkey and Vegetable Stir-Fry with Brown Rice
- Grilled Chicken Caesar Salad
- Veggie-Packed Egg White Frittata
- Lentil and Chickpea Salad with Lemon Vinaigrette
- Quinoa and Black Bean Veggie Burgers

Grilled Chicken Breast with Steamed Broccoli

Ingredients:

- 4 boneless, skinless chicken breasts
- 2 tablespoons olive oil
- 2 cloves garlic, minced
- 1 teaspoon dried oregano
- 1 teaspoon dried thyme
- Salt and pepper to taste
- 1 large head of broccoli, cut into florets
- Lemon wedges (for serving)

Instructions:

1. Marinate Chicken:
   In a bowl, mix together olive oil, minced garlic, dried oregano, dried thyme, salt, and pepper. Add chicken breasts to the marinade, making sure they are well coated. Let them marinate for at least 30 minutes in the refrigerator.
2. Preheat Grill:
   Preheat your grill to medium-high heat.
3. Grill Chicken:
   Remove chicken breasts from the marinade and discard excess marinade. Place chicken breasts on the preheated grill. Grill for 6-7 minutes on each side, or until the internal temperature reaches 165°F (75°C) and the chicken is no longer pink in the center.
4. Steam Broccoli:
   While the chicken is grilling, steam the broccoli florets. Place them in a steamer basket over a pot of boiling water. Cover and steam for 5-7 minutes, or until the broccoli is tender but still crisp.
5. Serve:
   Serve the grilled chicken breasts with steamed broccoli on the side. Squeeze fresh lemon juice over the chicken and broccoli before serving, if desired.
6. Enjoy!
   Enjoy this healthy and delicious Grilled Chicken Breast with Steamed Broccoli as a nutritious meal.

Baked Salmon with Asparagus

Ingredients:

- 4 salmon fillets, skin-on or skinless, about 6 oz each
- 1 bunch asparagus, woody ends trimmed
- 2 tablespoons olive oil
- 2 cloves garlic, minced
- 1 teaspoon lemon zest
- 1 tablespoon lemon juice
- Salt and pepper to taste
- Optional garnish: chopped fresh parsley, lemon slices

Instructions:

1. Preheat Oven:
   Preheat your oven to 400°F (200°C). Line a baking sheet with parchment paper or aluminum foil for easy cleanup.
2. Prepare Salmon:
   Pat the salmon fillets dry with paper towels and place them on the prepared baking sheet. If using skin-on salmon, arrange them skin-side down. Season the salmon fillets with salt and pepper to taste.
3. Prepare Asparagus:
   Place trimmed asparagus spears on the baking sheet around the salmon fillets.
4. Make Lemon Garlic Mixture:
   In a small bowl, whisk together olive oil, minced garlic, lemon zest, and lemon juice. Drizzle the mixture over the salmon fillets and asparagus.
5. Bake:
   Place the baking sheet in the preheated oven and bake for 12-15 minutes, or until the salmon is cooked through and flakes easily with a fork, and the asparagus is tender but still crisp.
6. Serve:
   Remove the baked salmon and asparagus from the oven. Optionally, garnish with chopped fresh parsley and lemon slices.
7. Enjoy!
   Serve the Baked Salmon with Asparagus hot as a delicious and nutritious meal.

This Baked Salmon with Asparagus recipe is quick and easy to make, yet elegant enough for a special occasion. It's a healthy and flavorful dish that's perfect for busy weeknights or entertaining guests. Enjoy the tender and flaky salmon paired with the vibrant and crisp asparagus, all infused with the bright flavors of lemon and garlic.

Turkey and Quinoa Stuffed Bell Peppers

Ingredients:

- 4 large bell peppers, any color
- 1 cup quinoa, rinsed
- 1 lb lean ground turkey
- 1 tablespoon olive oil
- 1 onion, diced
- 2 cloves garlic, minced
- 1 can (14.5 oz) diced tomatoes, drained
- 1 cup low-sodium chicken or vegetable broth
- 1 teaspoon dried oregano
- 1 teaspoon dried basil
- 1/2 teaspoon paprika
- Salt and pepper to taste
- 1 cup shredded mozzarella or cheddar cheese
- Fresh parsley or cilantro, chopped (for garnish)

Instructions:

1. Preheat Oven:
   Preheat your oven to 375°F (190°C). Grease a baking dish large enough to hold the bell peppers upright.
2. Prepare Bell Peppers:
   Slice the tops off the bell peppers and remove the seeds and membranes. If necessary, slice a thin layer from the bottom of each pepper so they stand upright. Place the peppers in the prepared baking dish.
3. Cook Quinoa:
   In a saucepan, combine quinoa with 2 cups of water. Bring to a boil, then reduce heat to low, cover, and simmer for 15-20 minutes, or until quinoa is cooked and water is absorbed.
4. Cook Turkey Mixture:
   In a large skillet, heat olive oil over medium heat. Add diced onion and minced garlic, and cook until softened, about 3-4 minutes. Add ground turkey and cook until browned, breaking it up with a spoon as it cooks. Drain any excess fat if needed.

5. Add Tomatoes and Seasonings:
   Stir in diced tomatoes (drained), chicken or vegetable broth, dried oregano, dried basil, paprika, salt, and pepper. Let the mixture simmer for 5-7 minutes, allowing flavors to meld together.
6. Combine Turkey Mixture with Quinoa:
   Add cooked quinoa to the skillet with the turkey mixture. Stir well to combine.
7. Stuff Bell Peppers:
   Spoon the turkey and quinoa mixture into the hollowed-out bell peppers until they are full. Press down gently to pack the filling.
8. Bake:
   Sprinkle shredded cheese over the stuffed bell peppers. Cover the baking dish with aluminum foil and bake in the preheated oven for 25-30 minutes.
9. Broil (Optional):
   Remove the foil and broil for an additional 3-5 minutes, or until the cheese is golden and bubbly.
10. Serve:
    Remove the stuffed bell peppers from the oven and let them cool slightly. Garnish with chopped fresh parsley or cilantro before serving.
11. Enjoy!
    Serve the Turkey and Quinoa Stuffed Bell Peppers hot as a flavorful and nutritious meal.

Spicy Tofu Stir-Fry with Brown Rice

Ingredients:

For the Stir-Fry Sauce:

- 1/4 cup low-sodium soy sauce
- 2 tablespoons rice vinegar
- 1 tablespoon hoisin sauce
- 1 tablespoon sriracha sauce (adjust to taste)
- 1 tablespoon sesame oil
- 2 cloves garlic, minced
- 1 teaspoon grated ginger
- 1 teaspoon cornstarch

For the Stir-Fry:

- 14 oz (400g) extra-firm tofu, drained and pressed
- 2 tablespoons cornstarch
- 2 tablespoons vegetable oil
- 1 red bell pepper, sliced
- 1 green bell pepper, sliced
- 1 small onion, sliced
- 2 cups broccoli florets
- Cooked brown rice, for serving
- Optional garnish: sliced green onions, sesame seeds

Instructions:

1. Prepare the Stir-Fry Sauce:
   In a small bowl, whisk together soy sauce, rice vinegar, hoisin sauce, sriracha sauce, sesame oil, minced garlic, grated ginger, and cornstarch. Set aside.
2. Prepare the Tofu:
   Cut the pressed tofu into cubes. Place them in a bowl and toss with cornstarch until evenly coated.

3. Cook the Tofu:
   Heat vegetable oil in a large skillet or wok over medium-high heat. Add the tofu cubes and cook until golden and crispy on all sides, about 5-7 minutes. Remove tofu from the skillet and set aside.
4. Cook the Vegetables:
   In the same skillet, add a little more oil if needed. Add sliced bell peppers, onion, and broccoli florets. Stir-fry for 5-6 minutes, or until the vegetables are tender-crisp.
5. Combine:
   Return the cooked tofu to the skillet with the vegetables. Pour the prepared stir-fry sauce over the tofu and vegetables. Stir well to coat everything evenly in the sauce.
6. Simmer:
   Let the stir-fry simmer for 2-3 minutes, or until the sauce has thickened slightly.
7. Serve:
   Serve the Spicy Tofu Stir-Fry hot over cooked brown rice. Garnish with sliced green onions and sesame seeds if desired.
8. Enjoy!
   Enjoy this delicious and spicy tofu stir-fry with brown rice for a flavorful and nutritious meal! Adjust the level of spiciness according to your preference.

Egg White Omelette with Spinach and Mushrooms

Ingredients:

- 4 large egg whites
- 1 cup fresh spinach leaves, chopped
- 1/2 cup mushrooms, sliced
- 1/4 cup diced onion
- 1 tablespoon olive oil
- Salt and pepper to taste
- Optional toppings: shredded cheese, diced tomatoes, avocado slices

Instructions:

1. Prepare the Vegetables:
   Heat olive oil in a non-stick skillet over medium heat. Add diced onion and sliced mushrooms. Cook for 3-4 minutes, or until the vegetables are softened.
2. Add Spinach:
   Add chopped spinach to the skillet with the mushrooms and onions. Cook for an additional 1-2 minutes, or until the spinach is wilted. Season with salt and pepper to taste.
3. Whisk Egg Whites:
   In a separate bowl, whisk the egg whites until frothy.
4. Cook the Omelette:
   Pour the whisked egg whites evenly over the cooked vegetables in the skillet. Allow the omelette to cook undisturbed for a few minutes until the edges start to set.
5. Fold and Finish:
   Gently lift the edges of the omelette with a spatula and tilt the skillet to allow any uncooked egg whites to flow to the bottom. Once the omelette is mostly set but still slightly runny on top, carefully fold it in half with the spatula.
6. Cook Through:
   Continue cooking the omelette for another 1-2 minutes, or until the egg whites are fully cooked and no longer runny.
7. Serve:
   Slide the cooked omelette onto a plate and serve hot. Optionally, top with shredded cheese, diced tomatoes, or avocado slices for extra flavor and texture.

8. Enjoy!
   Enjoy this delicious and healthy Egg White Omelette with Spinach and Mushrooms as a nutritious breakfast or brunch option. It's low in calories and high in protein, making it perfect for a fitness-focused meal plan.

Greek Yogurt Parfait with Fresh Berries and Granola

Ingredients:

- 1 cup Greek yogurt (plain or vanilla flavored)
- 1/2 cup fresh berries (such as strawberries, blueberries, raspberries)
- 1/4 cup granola (homemade or store-bought)
- 1 tablespoon honey or maple syrup (optional, for added sweetness)
- Fresh mint leaves (for garnish, optional)

Instructions:

1. Prepare Ingredients:
   Wash and dry the fresh berries. If using strawberries, hull and slice them into smaller pieces.
2. Layer Yogurt:
   Start by spooning a layer of Greek yogurt into the bottom of a glass or bowl.
3. Add Berries:
   Add a layer of fresh berries on top of the yogurt. You can use a single type of berry or a combination of different berries for variety.
4. Sprinkle Granola:
   Sprinkle a layer of granola over the berries. You can use your favorite granola variety, such as plain, honey almond, or mixed berry granola.
5. Repeat Layers:
   Repeat the layers of yogurt, berries, and granola until you reach the top of the glass or bowl, ending with a final layer of granola on top.
6. Drizzle with Honey or Maple Syrup:
   If desired, drizzle a little honey or maple syrup over the top of the parfait for added sweetness. This step is optional, especially if your Greek yogurt is already sweetened.
7. Garnish:
   Garnish the parfait with a few fresh mint leaves for a pop of color and added freshness, if desired.
8. Serve:
   Serve the Greek Yogurt Parfait with Fresh Berries and Granola immediately as a delicious and nutritious breakfast, snack, or dessert option.

9. Enjoy!
   Enjoy this light and refreshing parfait, packed with protein from the Greek yogurt, fiber from the berries, and crunch from the granola. It's a satisfying and healthy treat for any time of day!

Quinoa and Black Bean Salad with Avocado

Ingredients:

- 1 cup quinoa, rinsed
- 1 can (15 oz) black beans, drained and rinsed
- 1 ripe avocado, diced
- 1 cup cherry tomatoes, halved
- 1/2 cup red onion, finely chopped
- 1/4 cup fresh cilantro, chopped
- Juice of 1 lime
- 2 tablespoons olive oil
- 1 teaspoon ground cumin
- Salt and pepper to taste
- Optional: diced jalapeño for heat, crumbled feta cheese for garnish

Instructions:

1. Cook Quinoa:
   In a medium saucepan, combine quinoa with 2 cups of water. Bring to a boil, then reduce heat to low, cover, and simmer for 15-20 minutes, or until quinoa is cooked and water is absorbed. Fluff with a fork and let it cool.
2. Prepare Dressing:
   In a small bowl, whisk together lime juice, olive oil, ground cumin, salt, and pepper to make the dressing.
3. Assemble Salad:
   In a large mixing bowl, combine cooked quinoa, black beans, diced avocado, halved cherry tomatoes, finely chopped red onion, and chopped cilantro.
4. Add Dressing:
   Pour the prepared dressing over the quinoa and black bean mixture. Toss gently until everything is well coated in the dressing.
5. Chill:
   Cover the bowl and refrigerate the salad for at least 30 minutes to allow the flavors to meld together.
6. Serve:
   Once chilled, give the salad a final toss and taste for seasoning. Adjust salt and pepper if needed. Optionally, garnish with diced jalapeño for extra heat and crumbled feta cheese for added flavor.

7. Enjoy!
   Serve the Quinoa and Black Bean Salad with Avocado as a light and refreshing meal on its own, or as a side dish to accompany grilled meats or fish. It's perfect for picnics, potlucks, or as a healthy lunch option.

Lean Beef Stir-Fry with Mixed Vegetables

Ingredients:

- 1 lb lean beef (such as flank steak or sirloin), thinly sliced against the grain
- 2 tablespoons soy sauce
- 2 tablespoons oyster sauce
- 1 tablespoon hoisin sauce
- 1 tablespoon cornstarch
- 2 tablespoons vegetable oil, divided
- 2 cloves garlic, minced
- 1 teaspoon grated ginger
- 1 onion, thinly sliced
- 1 bell pepper (any color), thinly sliced
- 1 cup broccoli florets
- 1 cup snap peas
- Salt and pepper to taste
- Cooked rice or noodles, for serving
- Optional garnish: sliced green onions, sesame seeds

Instructions:

1. Marinate Beef:
   In a bowl, combine soy sauce, oyster sauce, hoisin sauce, and cornstarch. Add the thinly sliced beef to the marinade and toss to coat. Let it marinate for at least 15 minutes.
2. Heat Oil:
   Heat 1 tablespoon of vegetable oil in a large skillet or wok over medium-high heat.
3. Cook Beef:
   Add the marinated beef to the skillet in a single layer. Cook for 2-3 minutes without stirring, allowing it to sear and develop a brown crust. Then, stir-fry for another 1-2 minutes until the beef is cooked through. Remove the beef from the skillet and set aside.
4. Cook Vegetables:
   In the same skillet, add the remaining tablespoon of vegetable oil. Add minced garlic and grated ginger, and cook for about 30 seconds until fragrant. Add thinly

sliced onion, bell pepper, broccoli florets, and snap peas. Stir-fry for 3-4 minutes, or until the vegetables are crisp-tender.
5. Combine:
Return the cooked beef to the skillet with the cooked vegetables. Stir everything together and cook for an additional minute to heat through. Season with salt and pepper to taste.
6. Serve:
Serve the Lean Beef Stir-Fry with Mixed Vegetables hot over cooked rice or noodles.
7. Garnish:
Optionally, garnish with sliced green onions and sesame seeds for added flavor and presentation.
8. Enjoy!
Enjoy this flavorful and nutritious stir-fry as a quick and satisfying meal for lunch or dinner.

Oven-Roasted Turkey Breast with Sweet Potatoes

Ingredients:

- 1 turkey breast (about 2-3 lbs), bone-in and skin-on
- 2-3 medium sweet potatoes, peeled and cut into chunks
- 2 tablespoons olive oil
- 2 cloves garlic, minced
- 1 teaspoon dried thyme
- 1 teaspoon dried rosemary
- 1 teaspoon dried sage
- Salt and pepper to taste
- Optional: 1/4 cup chicken or turkey broth

Instructions:

1. Preheat Oven:
   Preheat your oven to 375°F (190°C).
2. Prepare Turkey Breast:
   Pat the turkey breast dry with paper towels. Place it in a roasting pan or baking dish.
3. Prepare Sweet Potatoes:
   In a large bowl, toss the sweet potato chunks with olive oil, minced garlic, dried thyme, dried rosemary, dried sage, salt, and pepper until evenly coated.
4. Roast Turkey and Sweet Potatoes:
   Arrange the sweet potato chunks around the turkey breast in the roasting pan. If desired, pour chicken or turkey broth into the bottom of the pan for added moisture.
5. Season Turkey:
   Season the turkey breast generously with salt and pepper.
6. Roast:
   Place the roasting pan in the preheated oven. Roast for about 20 minutes per pound of turkey breast, or until the internal temperature reaches 165°F (75°C) when measured with a meat thermometer inserted into the thickest part of the breast.
7. Baste (Optional):
   If desired, baste the turkey breast and sweet potatoes with pan juices halfway through the cooking time to keep them moist.

8. Rest and Serve:
   Once the turkey breast is cooked through and the sweet potatoes are tender, remove the roasting pan from the oven. Tent the turkey breast with aluminum foil and let it rest for 10-15 minutes before slicing.
9. Slice and Serve:
   Carve the turkey breast into slices and serve with the roasted sweet potatoes on the side.
10. Enjoy!
    Enjoy this delicious Oven-Roasted Turkey Breast with Sweet Potatoes as a comforting and nutritious meal, perfect for any occasion!

Shrimp and Vegetable Skewers with Quinoa

Ingredients:

For the Shrimp Skewers:

- 1 lb large shrimp, peeled and deveined
- 2 tablespoons olive oil
- 2 cloves garlic, minced
- 1 teaspoon paprika
- 1/2 teaspoon dried oregano
- Salt and pepper to taste
- Wooden or metal skewers

For the Vegetable Skewers:

- 1 bell pepper, cut into chunks
- 1 zucchini, sliced
- 1 yellow squash, sliced
- 1 red onion, cut into chunks
- Cherry tomatoes
- 2 tablespoons olive oil
- Salt and pepper to taste

For the Quinoa:

- 1 cup quinoa, rinsed
- 2 cups water or vegetable broth
- Salt to taste

Instructions:

1. Prepare Quinoa:
   In a medium saucepan, combine quinoa with water or vegetable broth and a pinch of salt. Bring to a boil, then reduce heat to low, cover, and simmer for 15-20 minutes, or until quinoa is cooked and liquid is absorbed. Fluff with a fork and set aside.

2. Marinate Shrimp:
   In a bowl, combine shrimp with olive oil, minced garlic, paprika, dried oregano, salt, and pepper. Toss until the shrimp are evenly coated. Let them marinate for at least 15 minutes.
3. Prepare Vegetables:
   In another bowl, toss the bell pepper chunks, zucchini slices, yellow squash slices, red onion chunks, and cherry tomatoes with olive oil, salt, and pepper until coated.
4. Assemble Skewers:
   Thread the marinated shrimp and prepared vegetables onto skewers, alternating between shrimp and vegetables.
5. Preheat Grill:
   Preheat your grill to medium-high heat.
6. Grill Skewers:
   Place the skewers on the preheated grill. Grill for 2-3 minutes on each side, or until the shrimp are pink and opaque and the vegetables are tender and slightly charred.
7. Serve:
   Serve the grilled Shrimp and Vegetable Skewers hot with cooked quinoa on the side.
8. Enjoy!
   Enjoy this delicious and nutritious meal of Shrimp and Vegetable Skewers with Quinoa, perfect for a summer barbecue or any time of year!

Chicken and Vegetable Curry with Brown Rice

Ingredients:

For the Curry:

- 1 lb boneless, skinless chicken breasts, cut into bite-sized pieces
- 2 tablespoons vegetable oil
- 1 onion, diced
- 3 cloves garlic, minced
- 1 tablespoon ginger, minced
- 2 tablespoons curry powder
- 1 teaspoon ground turmeric
- 1 teaspoon ground cumin
- 1 teaspoon ground coriander
- 1/2 teaspoon red pepper flakes (adjust to taste)
- 1 can (14 oz) coconut milk
- 1 cup chicken broth
- 2 cups mixed vegetables (such as bell peppers, carrots, peas, and potatoes), diced
- Salt and pepper to taste
- Fresh cilantro, chopped (for garnish)

For the Brown Rice:

- 1 cup brown rice
- 2 cups water or chicken broth
- Salt to taste

Instructions:

1. Cook Brown Rice:
   Rinse the brown rice under cold water until the water runs clear. In a medium saucepan, combine the brown rice with water or chicken broth and a pinch of salt. Bring to a boil, then reduce heat to low, cover, and simmer for 45-50 minutes, or until the rice is cooked and liquid is absorbed. Fluff with a fork and set aside.
2. Prepare Chicken and Vegetables:
   Heat vegetable oil in a large skillet or Dutch oven over medium heat. Add diced

onion and cook until softened, about 3-4 minutes. Add minced garlic and ginger, and cook for an additional 1-2 minutes until fragrant.

3. Add Spices:

    Stir in curry powder, ground turmeric, ground cumin, ground coriander, and red pepper flakes. Cook for 1 minute until the spices are fragrant.

4. Cook Chicken:

    Add the bite-sized chicken pieces to the skillet and cook until browned on all sides, about 5-6 minutes.

5. Add Coconut Milk and Broth:

    Pour in the coconut milk and chicken broth. Bring the mixture to a simmer.

6. Add Vegetables:

    Add the diced mixed vegetables to the skillet. Stir well to combine.

7. Simmer:

    Reduce heat to low and let the curry simmer for 15-20 minutes, or until the chicken is cooked through and the vegetables are tender.

8. Season:

    Season the curry with salt and pepper to taste.

9. Serve:

    Serve the Chicken and Vegetable Curry hot over cooked brown rice.

10. Garnish:

    Garnish with freshly chopped cilantro before serving.

11. Enjoy!

    Enjoy this flavorful and aromatic Chicken and Vegetable Curry with Brown Rice as a comforting and satisfying meal! Adjust the level of spice according to your preference.

Veggie-Packed Turkey Chili

Ingredients:

- 1 lb ground turkey
- 1 tablespoon olive oil
- 1 onion, diced
- 2 cloves garlic, minced
- 1 bell pepper, diced
- 1 zucchini, diced
- 1 carrot, diced
- 1 can (14 oz) diced tomatoes
- 1 can (15 oz) kidney beans, drained and rinsed
- 1 can (15 oz) black beans, drained and rinsed
- 1 cup corn kernels (fresh, frozen, or canned)
- 1 tablespoon chili powder
- 1 teaspoon ground cumin
- 1/2 teaspoon paprika
- Salt and pepper to taste
- 3 cups chicken or vegetable broth
- Optional toppings: shredded cheese, chopped green onions, sour cream, avocado slices, cilantro

Instructions:

1. Cook Ground Turkey:
   Heat olive oil in a large pot or Dutch oven over medium heat. Add ground turkey and cook until browned, breaking it up with a spoon as it cooks.
2. Add Aromatics:
   Add diced onion and minced garlic to the pot with the browned turkey. Cook for 2-3 minutes until the onion is softened and aromatic.
3. Add Vegetables:
   Stir in diced bell pepper, diced zucchini, and diced carrot. Cook for another 3-4 minutes, stirring occasionally, until the vegetables are slightly softened.
4. Seasonings:
   Add chili powder, ground cumin, paprika, salt, and pepper to the pot. Stir well to coat the turkey and vegetables with the seasonings.

5. Add Tomatoes and Beans:
   Pour in the diced tomatoes (with their juices), drained and rinsed kidney beans, drained and rinsed black beans, and corn kernels. Stir to combine.
6. Add Broth:
   Pour in the chicken or vegetable broth. Bring the chili to a simmer.
7. Simmer:
   Reduce heat to low and let the chili simmer for 20-25 minutes, stirring occasionally, until the flavors meld together and the chili thickens slightly.
8. Adjust Seasoning:
   Taste the chili and adjust seasoning with more salt, pepper, or chili powder if needed.
9. Serve:
   Ladle the Veggie-Packed Turkey Chili into bowls. Serve hot with your favorite toppings such as shredded cheese, chopped green onions, sour cream, avocado slices, or cilantro.
10. Enjoy!
    Enjoy this delicious and nutritious Veggie-Packed Turkey Chili as a comforting meal on a cold day or anytime you're craving a hearty and satisfying dish!

Baked Cod with Lemon and Herbs

Ingredients:

- 4 cod fillets (about 6 oz each)
- 2 tablespoons olive oil
- 2 cloves garlic, minced
- Zest of 1 lemon
- Juice of 1 lemon
- 1 tablespoon fresh parsley, chopped
- 1 tablespoon fresh dill, chopped
- Salt and pepper to taste
- Lemon slices (for garnish)
- Fresh herbs (for garnish)

Instructions:

1. Preheat Oven:
   Preheat your oven to 400°F (200°C). Line a baking sheet with parchment paper or lightly grease it with olive oil.
2. Prepare Cod Fillets:
   Pat the cod fillets dry with paper towels. Place them on the prepared baking sheet, leaving space between each fillet.
3. Make Herb Mixture:
   In a small bowl, combine olive oil, minced garlic, lemon zest, lemon juice, chopped parsley, chopped dill, salt, and pepper. Mix well to combine.
4. Coat Cod Fillets:
   Spoon the herb mixture over the top of each cod fillet, spreading it evenly to coat the surface.
5. Bake:
   Place the baking sheet in the preheated oven and bake for 12-15 minutes, or until the cod is opaque and flakes easily with a fork.
6. Garnish:
   Remove the baked cod from the oven. Garnish with lemon slices and fresh herbs, such as parsley or dill, for an extra burst of flavor and freshness.

7. Serve:
   Serve the Baked Cod with Lemon and Herbs hot, with your choice of side dishes such as steamed vegetables, rice, or a fresh salad.
8. Enjoy!
   Enjoy this delicious and healthy Baked Cod with Lemon and Herbs as a light and flavorful meal, perfect for a quick weeknight dinner or a special occasion.

Tofu and Vegetable Stir-Fry with Quinoa

Ingredients:

For the Stir-Fry:

- 14 oz (400g) firm tofu, pressed and cubed
- 2 tablespoons soy sauce
- 1 tablespoon sesame oil
- 2 cloves garlic, minced
- 1 tablespoon grated ginger
- 1 bell pepper, thinly sliced
- 1 carrot, julienned
- 1 cup broccoli florets
- 1 cup snap peas
- 2 green onions, chopped
- 2 tablespoons vegetable oil, for cooking
- Salt and pepper to taste

For the Quinoa:

- 1 cup quinoa, rinsed
- 2 cups water or vegetable broth
- Salt to taste

For the Sauce:

- 1/4 cup soy sauce
- 2 tablespoons hoisin sauce
- 1 tablespoon rice vinegar
- 1 tablespoon maple syrup or honey
- 1 teaspoon cornstarch (optional, for thickening)

Instructions:

1. Cook Quinoa:
   In a medium saucepan, combine quinoa with water or vegetable broth and a pinch of salt. Bring to a boil, then reduce heat to low, cover, and simmer for 15-20 minutes, or until quinoa is cooked and liquid is absorbed. Fluff with a fork and set aside.
2. Prepare Tofu:
   Press the tofu to remove excess moisture. Cut the tofu into cubes and marinate in soy sauce and sesame oil for at least 15 minutes.
3. Make Sauce:
   In a small bowl, whisk together soy sauce, hoisin sauce, rice vinegar, and maple syrup (or honey). If you prefer a thicker sauce, add cornstarch and whisk until dissolved.
4. Stir-Fry Tofu:
   Heat vegetable oil in a large skillet or wok over medium-high heat. Add marinated tofu cubes and cook until golden brown on all sides. Remove tofu from the skillet and set aside.
5. Sauté Vegetables:
   In the same skillet, add a little more oil if needed. Add minced garlic and grated ginger, and cook for about 30 seconds until fragrant. Add sliced bell pepper, julienned carrot, broccoli florets, and snap peas. Stir-fry for 3-4 minutes, or until the vegetables are tender-crisp.
6. Combine Tofu and Sauce:
   Return the cooked tofu to the skillet with the sautéed vegetables. Pour the sauce over the tofu and vegetables. Stir well to coat everything evenly in the sauce.
7. Simmer:
   Let the stir-fry simmer for 2-3 minutes, or until the sauce has thickened slightly.
8. Serve:
   Serve the Tofu and Vegetable Stir-Fry hot over cooked quinoa.
9. Garnish:
   Garnish with chopped green onions before serving.
10. Enjoy!
    Enjoy this delicious and nutritious Tofu and Vegetable Stir-Fry with Quinoa as a wholesome and satisfying meal! Adjust the vegetables and sauce according to your taste preferences.

Grilled Steak Salad with Balsamic Vinaigrette

Ingredients:

For the Steak:

- 1 lb steak (such as flank steak, sirloin, or ribeye)
- 2 tablespoons olive oil
- 2 cloves garlic, minced
- 1 teaspoon dried thyme
- 1 teaspoon dried rosemary
- Salt and pepper to taste

For the Salad:

- Mixed salad greens (such as lettuce, spinach, arugula)
- Cherry tomatoes, halved
- Cucumber, sliced
- Red onion, thinly sliced
- Crumbled feta cheese
- Optional add-ons: avocado slices, grilled vegetables, nuts, seeds

For the Balsamic Vinaigrette:

- 1/4 cup balsamic vinegar
- 1/4 cup olive oil
- 1 tablespoon Dijon mustard
- 1 clove garlic, minced
- 1 teaspoon honey or maple syrup
- Salt and pepper to taste

Instructions:

1. Marinate Steak:
   In a bowl, combine olive oil, minced garlic, dried thyme, dried rosemary, salt, and pepper. Place the steak in the marinade, turning to coat both sides. Let it marinate for at least 30 minutes, or overnight in the refrigerator for best flavor.

2. Preheat Grill:
   Preheat your grill to medium-high heat.
3. Grill Steak:
   Remove the steak from the marinade and discard any excess marinade. Grill the steak for 4-6 minutes per side, or until it reaches your desired level of doneness. For medium-rare, the internal temperature should be around 130-135°F (54-57°C). Let the steak rest for a few minutes before slicing.
4. Prepare Salad:
   Meanwhile, prepare the salad ingredients. In a large bowl, combine mixed salad greens, halved cherry tomatoes, sliced cucumber, thinly sliced red onion, and crumbled feta cheese. Add any optional add-ons you like.
5. Make Balsamic Vinaigrette:
   In a small bowl, whisk together balsamic vinegar, olive oil, Dijon mustard, minced garlic, honey or maple syrup, salt, and pepper until well combined.
6. Slice Steak:
   Slice the grilled steak thinly against the grain.
7. Assemble Salad:
   Add the sliced steak to the salad bowl. Drizzle the balsamic vinaigrette over the salad and steak.
8. Toss:
   Gently toss everything together until the salad is evenly coated with the dressing.
9. Serve:
   Serve the Grilled Steak Salad with Balsamic Vinaigrette immediately, garnished with additional crumbled feta cheese and freshly cracked black pepper if desired.
10. Enjoy!
    Enjoy this delicious and satisfying Grilled Steak Salad with Balsamic Vinaigrette as a flavorful and nutritious meal! It's perfect for a light lunch or dinner.

Seared Tuna Nicoise Salad

Ingredients:

For the Salad:

- 8 oz fresh tuna steaks
- 4 cups mixed salad greens (such as lettuce, spinach, arugula)
- 1 cup cherry tomatoes, halved
- 1 cup boiled and halved baby potatoes
- 1 cup blanched green beans
- 4 boiled eggs, halved
- 1/4 cup Niçoise olives
- 2 tablespoons capers
- Optional: anchovy fillets, peeled and boiled shrimp

For the Dressing:

- 1/4 cup extra virgin olive oil
- 2 tablespoons red wine vinegar
- 1 tablespoon Dijon mustard
- 1 clove garlic, minced
- Salt and pepper to taste

Instructions:

1. Prepare Tuna:
   Pat the tuna steaks dry with paper towels. Season both sides with salt and pepper.
2. Sear Tuna:
   Heat a skillet or grill pan over high heat. Add a small amount of oil to the skillet. Once hot, sear the tuna steaks for 1-2 minutes on each side, or until desired doneness. The tuna should be seared on the outside but still pink in the center. Remove from heat and let it rest for a few minutes before slicing.
3. Prepare Salad Ingredients:
   Arrange the mixed salad greens on a large serving platter or individual plates. Arrange the halved cherry tomatoes, boiled baby potatoes, blanched green beans,

boiled eggs, Niçoise olives, capers, and any optional ingredients (such as anchovy fillets or boiled shrimp) around the greens.

4. Make Dressing:

    In a small bowl, whisk together the extra virgin olive oil, red wine vinegar, Dijon mustard, minced garlic, salt, and pepper until well combined.

5. Slice Tuna:

    Slice the seared tuna steaks into thin slices.

6. Assemble Salad:

    Arrange the sliced tuna over the salad ingredients.

7. Drizzle Dressing:

    Drizzle the dressing over the salad.

8. Serve:

    Serve the Seared Tuna Niçoise Salad immediately, garnished with additional freshly cracked black pepper if desired.

9. Enjoy!

    Enjoy this delicious and satisfying Seared Tuna Niçoise Salad as a light and flavorful meal, perfect for lunch or dinner.

Baked Chicken Thighs with Roasted Brussels Sprouts

Ingredients:

For the Chicken Thighs:

- 4 bone-in, skin-on chicken thighs
- 2 tablespoons olive oil
- 2 cloves garlic, minced
- 1 teaspoon paprika
- 1 teaspoon dried thyme
- Salt and pepper to taste

For the Brussels Sprouts:

- 1 lb Brussels sprouts, trimmed and halved
- 2 tablespoons olive oil
- Salt and pepper to taste
- Optional: balsamic glaze or grated Parmesan cheese for serving

Instructions:

1. Preheat Oven:
   Preheat your oven to 400°F (200°C). Line a baking sheet with parchment paper or lightly grease it with olive oil.
2. Prepare Chicken Thighs:
   In a small bowl, mix together olive oil, minced garlic, paprika, dried thyme, salt, and pepper. Pat the chicken thighs dry with paper towels and rub the spice mixture all over the chicken thighs.
3. Arrange Chicken and Brussels Sprouts:
   Place the seasoned chicken thighs on one side of the prepared baking sheet, skin side up. Arrange the halved Brussels sprouts on the other side of the baking sheet.
4. Drizzle with Olive Oil:
   Drizzle the Brussels sprouts with olive oil and season with salt and pepper to taste. Toss to coat evenly.

5. Bake:
   Transfer the baking sheet to the preheated oven and bake for 25-30 minutes, or until the chicken thighs are golden brown and crispy, and the Brussels sprouts are tender and caramelized.
6. Check Doneness:
   Check the internal temperature of the chicken thighs using a meat thermometer. It should register at least 165°F (74°C) in the thickest part of the thigh.
7. Serve:
   Once cooked through, remove the baking sheet from the oven. Allow the chicken thighs to rest for a few minutes before serving.
8. Optional Garnish:
   If desired, drizzle the chicken thighs and Brussels sprouts with balsamic glaze or sprinkle with grated Parmesan cheese before serving.
9. Enjoy!
   Serve the Baked Chicken Thighs with Roasted Brussels Sprouts hot as a delicious and satisfying meal. Enjoy the crispy skin of the chicken thighs alongside the flavorful roasted Brussels sprouts!

Lentil and Vegetable Soup

Ingredients:

- 1 cup dry lentils, rinsed and drained
- 1 tablespoon olive oil
- 1 onion, chopped
- 2 carrots, diced
- 2 celery stalks, diced
- 3 cloves garlic, minced
- 1 can (14 oz) diced tomatoes
- 4 cups vegetable broth
- 2 cups water
- 1 teaspoon dried thyme
- 1 teaspoon dried oregano
- 1 bay leaf
- Salt and pepper to taste
- 2 cups chopped fresh spinach or kale
- Juice of 1 lemon
- Fresh parsley, chopped (for garnish)
- Optional: grated Parmesan cheese, for serving

Instructions:

1. Prepare Lentils:
   Rinse the lentils under cold water and drain them. Set aside.
2. Sauté Vegetables:
   In a large pot or Dutch oven, heat olive oil over medium heat. Add chopped onion, diced carrots, and diced celery. Sauté for 5-7 minutes, or until the vegetables are softened.
3. Add Garlic and Spices:
   Add minced garlic to the pot and cook for another minute until fragrant. Stir in dried thyme, dried oregano, and bay leaf.
4. Add Lentils and Liquid:
   Add the rinsed and drained lentils to the pot. Pour in diced tomatoes (with their juices), vegetable broth, and water. Stir to combine.

5. Simmer:
   Bring the soup to a boil, then reduce heat to low. Cover and simmer for 20-25 minutes, or until the lentils are tender.
6. Season:
   Season the soup with salt and pepper to taste.
7. Add Greens and Lemon Juice:
   Stir in chopped fresh spinach or kale and lemon juice. Cook for an additional 2-3 minutes until the greens are wilted.
8. Adjust Consistency (Optional):
   If the soup is too thick, you can add more water or vegetable broth to reach your desired consistency.
9. Serve:
   Ladle the Lentil and Vegetable Soup into bowls. Garnish with freshly chopped parsley and grated Parmesan cheese if desired.
10. Enjoy!
    Serve this delicious and nutritious Lentil and Vegetable Soup hot as a comforting meal on a chilly day. It's packed with protein, fiber, and vitamins, making it a satisfying and wholesome dish.

Teriyaki Salmon with Stir-Fried Vegetables

Ingredients:

For the Teriyaki Salmon:

- 4 salmon fillets (about 6 oz each), skin-on or skinless
- 1/4 cup soy sauce
- 2 tablespoons honey or maple syrup
- 2 tablespoons rice vinegar
- 2 cloves garlic, minced
- 1 teaspoon grated ginger
- 1 tablespoon sesame oil
- 1 tablespoon cornstarch (optional, for thickening)
- Sesame seeds and chopped green onions for garnish

For the Stir-Fried Vegetables:

- 2 tablespoons vegetable oil
- 2 cups mixed vegetables (such as bell peppers, broccoli, carrots, snap peas, mushrooms), sliced or chopped
- 2 cloves garlic, minced
- 1 teaspoon grated ginger
- Salt and pepper to taste

Instructions:

1. Prepare Teriyaki Marinade:
   In a small bowl, whisk together soy sauce, honey or maple syrup, rice vinegar, minced garlic, grated ginger, sesame oil, and cornstarch (if using). Set aside.
2. Marinate Salmon:
   Place the salmon fillets in a shallow dish or resealable plastic bag. Pour the teriyaki marinade over the salmon, making sure it's evenly coated. Marinate in the refrigerator for at least 30 minutes, or up to 2 hours for maximum flavor.
3. Preheat Oven:
   Preheat your oven to 400°F (200°C). Line a baking sheet with parchment paper or lightly grease it with oil.

4. Bake Salmon:
   Remove the salmon fillets from the marinade, reserving the marinade for later. Place the salmon fillets on the prepared baking sheet. Bake in the preheated oven for 12-15 minutes, or until the salmon is cooked through and flakes easily with a fork.
5. Prepare Stir-Fried Vegetables:
   While the salmon is baking, heat vegetable oil in a large skillet or wok over medium-high heat. Add minced garlic and grated ginger, and cook for about 30 seconds until fragrant. Add the mixed vegetables to the skillet and stir-fry for 5-7 minutes, or until they are tender-crisp. Season with salt and pepper to taste.
6. Make Teriyaki Glaze:
   While the vegetables are cooking, transfer the reserved teriyaki marinade to a small saucepan. Bring to a simmer over medium heat and cook for 3-5 minutes, or until the sauce thickens slightly.
7. Serve:
   Once the salmon is cooked, remove it from the oven. Brush the salmon fillets with the prepared teriyaki glaze. Serve the Teriyaki Salmon hot with the stir-fried vegetables on the side.
8. Garnish:
   Garnish the salmon with sesame seeds and chopped green onions before serving.
9. Enjoy!
   Enjoy this delicious and flavorful Teriyaki Salmon with Stir-Fried Vegetables as a wholesome and satisfying meal. It's perfect for a quick and easy weeknight dinner!

Quinoa and Vegetable Stuffed Bell Peppers

Ingredients:

- 4 large bell peppers, any color
- 1 cup quinoa, rinsed
- 2 cups vegetable broth or water
- 1 tablespoon olive oil
- 1 onion, diced
- 2 cloves garlic, minced
- 1 carrot, diced
- 1 zucchini, diced
- 1 cup diced tomatoes (fresh or canned)
- 1 teaspoon dried oregano
- 1 teaspoon dried basil
- Salt and pepper to taste
- 1 cup shredded cheese (such as cheddar or mozzarella), divided
- Fresh parsley or cilantro, chopped (for garnish)

Instructions:

1. Preheat Oven:
   Preheat your oven to 375°F (190°C). Lightly grease a baking dish large enough to hold the bell peppers.
2. Prepare Bell Peppers:
   Cut the tops off the bell peppers and remove the seeds and membranes. If necessary, slice a small portion off the bottom of each pepper to help them stand upright in the baking dish. Set aside.
3. Cook Quinoa:
   In a saucepan, combine quinoa and vegetable broth or water. Bring to a boil, then reduce heat to low, cover, and simmer for 15-20 minutes, or until quinoa is cooked and liquid is absorbed. Remove from heat and fluff with a fork.
4. Prepare Filling:
   In a large skillet, heat olive oil over medium heat. Add diced onion and garlic, and cook until softened, about 2-3 minutes. Add diced carrot and zucchini, and cook for another 5 minutes, or until vegetables are tender.

5. Add Tomatoes and Seasonings:
   Stir in diced tomatoes, dried oregano, dried basil, salt, and pepper. Cook for 2-3 minutes, then remove from heat.
6. Combine Quinoa and Vegetables:
   In a large bowl, combine cooked quinoa with the cooked vegetable mixture. Stir well to combine. Add half of the shredded cheese and mix until evenly distributed.
7. Stuff Bell Peppers:
   Spoon the quinoa and vegetable mixture into the prepared bell peppers, pressing down gently to pack the filling. Fill each pepper to the top. Place the stuffed peppers in the prepared baking dish.
8. Bake:
   Cover the baking dish with aluminum foil and bake in the preheated oven for 25-30 minutes, or until the peppers are tender.
9. Add Cheese and Bake:
   Remove the foil from the baking dish. Sprinkle the remaining shredded cheese over the tops of the stuffed peppers. Return the baking dish to the oven and bake for an additional 5-10 minutes, or until the cheese is melted and bubbly.
10. Garnish and Serve:
    Remove the stuffed peppers from the oven. Garnish with chopped parsley or cilantro before serving.
11. Enjoy!
    Serve these delicious Quinoa and Vegetable Stuffed Bell Peppers hot as a nutritious and satisfying meal. They're perfect for a meatless dinner option!

Turkey Meatballs with Zucchini Noodles

Ingredients:

For the Turkey Meatballs:

- 1 lb ground turkey
- 1/2 cup breadcrumbs
- 1/4 cup grated Parmesan cheese
- 1 egg
- 2 cloves garlic, minced
- 2 tablespoons fresh parsley, chopped
- 1 teaspoon dried oregano
- 1/2 teaspoon salt
- 1/4 teaspoon black pepper
- 2 tablespoons olive oil (for cooking)

For the Zucchini Noodles:

- 4 medium zucchini
- 2 tablespoons olive oil
- 2 cloves garlic, minced
- Salt and pepper to taste
- Optional: grated Parmesan cheese, chopped fresh basil or parsley (for garnish)

Instructions:

1. Prepare Turkey Meatballs:
    - In a large bowl, combine ground turkey, breadcrumbs, grated Parmesan cheese, egg, minced garlic, chopped parsley, dried oregano, salt, and black pepper.
    - Mix until well combined, but do not overmix.
    - Shape the mixture into meatballs, about 1 inch in diameter.
2. Cook Turkey Meatballs:
    - Heat olive oil in a large skillet over medium heat.
    - Add the meatballs to the skillet, making sure not to overcrowd them.

- Cook the meatballs for 8-10 minutes, turning occasionally, until browned on all sides and cooked through.
- Remove the meatballs from the skillet and set aside.

3. Prepare Zucchini Noodles:
    - Using a spiralizer or vegetable peeler, spiralize or julienne the zucchini into noodles.
    - Heat olive oil in the same skillet over medium heat.
    - Add minced garlic and cook for about 1 minute, until fragrant.
    - Add the zucchini noodles to the skillet and toss to coat in the garlic-infused oil.
    - Cook the zucchini noodles for 3-5 minutes, stirring occasionally, until just tender but still crisp.
    - Season with salt and pepper to taste.
4. Assemble Dish:
    - Serve the cooked zucchini noodles in bowls or on plates.
    - Top with the cooked turkey meatballs.
    - Garnish with grated Parmesan cheese and chopped fresh basil or parsley, if desired.
5. Enjoy!
Serve this delicious and healthy Turkey Meatballs with Zucchini Noodles as a nutritious and satisfying meal. It's low-carb, gluten-free, and packed with flavor!

Baked Sweet Potato Fries with Greek Yogurt Dip

Ingredients:

For the Sweet Potato Fries:

- 2 large sweet potatoes, washed and peeled
- 2 tablespoons olive oil
- 1 teaspoon paprika
- 1/2 teaspoon garlic powder
- 1/2 teaspoon onion powder
- 1/2 teaspoon salt
- 1/4 teaspoon black pepper
- Optional: chopped fresh parsley or cilantro for garnish

For the Greek Yogurt Dip:

- 1 cup Greek yogurt
- 1 tablespoon lemon juice
- 1 clove garlic, minced
- 1 tablespoon chopped fresh dill
- Salt and pepper to taste

Instructions:

1. Preheat Oven:
   Preheat your oven to 425°F (220°C). Line a baking sheet with parchment paper or lightly grease it with olive oil.
2. Cut Sweet Potatoes:
   Cut the sweet potatoes into thin fries, about 1/4 inch thick. Try to make them as uniform in size as possible for even baking.
3. Season Sweet Potato Fries:
   In a large bowl, toss the sweet potato fries with olive oil, paprika, garlic powder, onion powder, salt, and black pepper until evenly coated.

4. Arrange Fries on Baking Sheet:
   Arrange the seasoned sweet potato fries in a single layer on the prepared baking sheet, making sure they are not overcrowded.
5. Bake:
   Bake the sweet potato fries in the preheated oven for 20-25 minutes, flipping halfway through, until they are crispy and golden brown.
6. Prepare Greek Yogurt Dip:
   While the sweet potato fries are baking, prepare the Greek yogurt dip. In a small bowl, mix together Greek yogurt, lemon juice, minced garlic, chopped fresh dill, salt, and pepper until well combined. Adjust seasoning to taste.
7. Serve:
   Once the sweet potato fries are done baking, remove them from the oven and let them cool slightly. Serve the baked sweet potato fries hot, garnished with chopped fresh parsley or cilantro if desired, alongside the Greek yogurt dip.
8. Enjoy!
   Enjoy these delicious Baked Sweet Potato Fries with Greek Yogurt Dip as a healthier alternative to traditional fries. They're perfect as a snack, appetizer, or side dish!

Chicken Caesar Salad with Whole Grain Croutons

Ingredients:

For the Salad:

- 2 boneless, skinless chicken breasts
- Salt and pepper to taste
- 1 tablespoon olive oil
- 1 head romaine lettuce, washed and chopped
- 1/4 cup grated Parmesan cheese
- Caesar salad dressing (store-bought or homemade)

For the Whole Grain Croutons:

- 2 cups whole grain bread, cubed
- 2 tablespoons olive oil
- 1 teaspoon garlic powder
- 1/2 teaspoon dried thyme
- Salt and pepper to taste

Instructions:

1. Prepare Chicken:
    - Season the chicken breasts with salt and pepper on both sides.
    - Heat olive oil in a skillet over medium-high heat.
    - Add the seasoned chicken breasts to the skillet and cook for 6-8 minutes on each side, or until cooked through and no longer pink in the center.
    - Remove the chicken from the skillet and let it rest for a few minutes before slicing.
2. Make Whole Grain Croutons:
    - Preheat your oven to 375°F (190°C).
    - In a bowl, toss the cubed whole grain bread with olive oil, garlic powder, dried thyme, salt, and pepper until well coated.
    - Spread the seasoned bread cubes in a single layer on a baking sheet.

- Bake in the preheated oven for 10-15 minutes, or until the croutons are golden brown and crispy. Keep an eye on them to prevent burning.
3. Assemble Salad:
    - In a large bowl, combine the chopped romaine lettuce with grated Parmesan cheese.
    - Add sliced chicken breast on top of the lettuce.
    - Drizzle Caesar salad dressing over the salad according to your taste preference.
    - Toss everything together until evenly coated with the dressing.
4. Add Croutons:
    - Once the croutons are done baking and slightly cooled, add them to the salad just before serving.
    - Toss the salad again to distribute the croutons evenly.
5. Serve:
    - Divide the Chicken Caesar Salad with Whole Grain Croutons among individual plates or bowls.
    - Serve immediately and enjoy!
6. Optional Additions:
    - Feel free to add additional toppings to your Chicken Caesar Salad, such as cherry tomatoes, sliced cucumbers, or sliced red onions, for extra flavor and crunch.
7. Enjoy!
Enjoy this delicious and satisfying Chicken Caesar Salad with Whole Grain Croutons as a nutritious meal option for lunch or dinner!

Vegetarian Lentil Sloppy Joes

Ingredients:

- 1 cup dried brown lentils
- 3 cups vegetable broth or water
- 1 tablespoon olive oil
- 1 onion, diced
- 2 cloves garlic, minced
- 1 bell pepper, diced
- 1 carrot, grated
- 1 celery stalk, diced
- 1 can (14 oz) diced tomatoes
- 2 tablespoons tomato paste
- 2 tablespoons soy sauce or tamari
- 1 tablespoon Worcestershire sauce (optional)
- 1 tablespoon maple syrup or brown sugar
- 1 teaspoon chili powder
- 1/2 teaspoon smoked paprika
- Salt and pepper to taste
- Hamburger buns or bread rolls, for serving

Instructions:

1. Cook Lentils:
    - Rinse the lentils under cold water and drain them.
    - In a saucepan, bring the vegetable broth or water to a boil.
    - Add the lentils to the boiling liquid, then reduce the heat to low, cover, and simmer for 20-25 minutes, or until the lentils are tender but not mushy. Drain any excess liquid and set the cooked lentils aside.
2. Prepare Vegetables:
    - Heat olive oil in a large skillet over medium heat.
    - Add diced onion and minced garlic to the skillet and cook until softened, about 3-4 minutes.
    - Add diced bell pepper, grated carrot, and diced celery to the skillet. Cook for another 5 minutes, or until the vegetables are tender.
3. Make Sloppy Joe Sauce:
    - Add the cooked lentils to the skillet with the cooked vegetables.

- Stir in diced tomatoes, tomato paste, soy sauce or tamari, Worcestershire sauce (if using), maple syrup or brown sugar, chili powder, smoked paprika, salt, and pepper.
- Mix well to combine all the ingredients.
- Simmer the mixture for 10-15 minutes, stirring occasionally, until the flavors are well blended and the sauce has thickened slightly.

4. Adjust Seasoning:
    - Taste the sloppy joe mixture and adjust the seasoning as needed, adding more salt, pepper, or spices to suit your taste preferences.
5. Assemble Sloppy Joes:
    - Toast the hamburger buns or bread rolls if desired.
    - Spoon the vegetarian lentil sloppy joe mixture onto the bottom halves of the buns.
    - Top with the other halves of the buns.
6. Serve:
    - Serve the Vegetarian Lentil Sloppy Joes immediately, with your favorite side dishes such as coleslaw, potato salad, or chips.
7. Enjoy!
    - Enjoy these delicious and hearty Vegetarian Lentil Sloppy Joes as a satisfying meatless meal option for lunch or dinner!

Grilled Veggie and Chicken Skewers

Ingredients:

For the Marinade:

- 1/4 cup olive oil
- 2 tablespoons balsamic vinegar
- 2 cloves garlic, minced
- 1 tablespoon honey or maple syrup
- 1 teaspoon dried Italian herbs (such as oregano, basil, thyme)
- Salt and pepper to taste

For the Skewers:

- 2 boneless, skinless chicken breasts, cut into 1-inch cubes
- 2 bell peppers, cut into chunks
- 1 zucchini, sliced
- 1 red onion, cut into chunks
- Cherry tomatoes
- Wooden or metal skewers (if using wooden skewers, soak them in water for 30 minutes before using)

Instructions:

1. Prepare Marinade:
    - In a small bowl, whisk together olive oil, balsamic vinegar, minced garlic, honey or maple syrup, dried Italian herbs, salt, and pepper until well combined. Set aside.
2. Marinate Chicken:
    - Place the chicken breast cubes in a shallow dish or resealable plastic bag.
    - Pour half of the marinade over the chicken, reserving the other half for the vegetables. Toss the chicken to coat evenly in the marinade.
    - Cover the dish or seal the bag and refrigerate for at least 30 minutes, or up to 2 hours to marinate.
3. Prepare Vegetables:
    - In another shallow dish or resealable plastic bag, place the prepared bell peppers, zucchini slices, red onion chunks, and cherry tomatoes.

- Pour the remaining marinade over the vegetables. Toss to coat evenly. Let the vegetables marinate while the chicken is marinating.

4. Assemble Skewers:
    - Preheat your grill to medium-high heat.
    - Thread the marinated chicken cubes and marinated vegetables onto the skewers, alternating between chicken and vegetables.
    - Make sure to leave a little space between each piece to ensure even cooking.

5. Grill Skewers:
    - Place the assembled skewers on the preheated grill.
    - Grill for 8-10 minutes, turning occasionally, or until the chicken is cooked through and the vegetables are tender and slightly charred.

6. Serve:
    - Once cooked, remove the skewers from the grill.
    - Transfer the Grilled Veggie and Chicken Skewers to a serving platter.
    - Garnish with chopped fresh herbs, if desired.

7. Enjoy!
    - Serve these delicious Grilled Veggie and Chicken Skewers hot as a flavorful and nutritious meal. They're perfect for summer gatherings or weeknight dinners!

Spaghetti Squash with Turkey Bolognese Sauce

Ingredients:

For the Spaghetti Squash:

- 1 large spaghetti squash
- Olive oil
- Salt and pepper to taste

For the Turkey Bolognese Sauce:

- 1 lb ground turkey
- 1 tablespoon olive oil
- 1 onion, diced
- 2 cloves garlic, minced
- 1 carrot, diced
- 1 celery stalk, diced
- 1 can (14 oz) crushed tomatoes
- 1/2 cup tomato paste
- 1/2 cup chicken or vegetable broth
- 1 teaspoon dried oregano
- 1 teaspoon dried basil
- Salt and pepper to taste
- Fresh parsley, chopped (for garnish)
- Grated Parmesan cheese (optional, for serving)

Instructions:

1. Prepare Spaghetti Squash:
    - Preheat your oven to 400°F (200°C).
    - Cut the spaghetti squash in half lengthwise and scoop out the seeds.
    - Drizzle the cut sides of the spaghetti squash with olive oil and season with salt and pepper.
    - Place the squash halves cut side down on a baking sheet lined with parchment paper.
    - Roast in the preheated oven for 35-45 minutes, or until the squash is tender and easily pierced with a fork.

- Remove the squash from the oven and let it cool slightly.
2. Prepare Turkey Bolognese Sauce:
    - While the spaghetti squash is roasting, heat olive oil in a large skillet over medium heat.
    - Add diced onion, minced garlic, diced carrot, and diced celery to the skillet. Cook until softened, about 5-7 minutes.
    - Add ground turkey to the skillet and cook until browned, breaking it up with a spoon as it cooks.
    - Stir in crushed tomatoes, tomato paste, chicken or vegetable broth, dried oregano, dried basil, salt, and pepper.
    - Bring the sauce to a simmer and let it cook for 15-20 minutes, stirring occasionally, until the flavors are well combined and the sauce has thickened.
3. Prepare Spaghetti Squash Strands:
    - Use a fork to scrape the flesh of the roasted spaghetti squash into strands. The flesh should easily come apart into strands resembling spaghetti noodles.
4. Assemble Dish:
    - Divide the spaghetti squash strands among serving plates.
    - Top each serving of spaghetti squash with a generous amount of turkey bolognese sauce.
5. Garnish and Serve:
    - Garnish the Spaghetti Squash with Turkey Bolognese Sauce with chopped fresh parsley and grated Parmesan cheese, if desired.
6. Enjoy!
    - Serve this delicious and satisfying dish hot as a wholesome and nutritious meal. Enjoy the flavors of the turkey bolognese sauce paired with the tender strands of spaghetti squash!

Turkey and Spinach Meatloaf

Ingredients:

- 1 lb ground turkey
- 1 cup fresh spinach, chopped
- 1/2 cup breadcrumbs
- 1/4 cup grated Parmesan cheese
- 1 small onion, finely chopped
- 2 cloves garlic, minced
- 1 large egg, lightly beaten
- 2 tablespoons Worcestershire sauce
- 1 tablespoon Dijon mustard
- 1 teaspoon dried oregano
- 1/2 teaspoon salt
- 1/4 teaspoon black pepper
- Olive oil (for greasing the baking dish)
- Ketchup or barbecue sauce (optional, for topping)

Instructions:

1. Preheat Oven:
   Preheat your oven to 375°F (190°C). Grease a loaf pan with olive oil or line it with parchment paper.
2. Mix Ingredients:
   - In a large mixing bowl, combine the ground turkey, chopped spinach, breadcrumbs, grated Parmesan cheese, finely chopped onion, minced garlic, lightly beaten egg, Worcestershire sauce, Dijon mustard, dried oregano, salt, and black pepper.
   - Use your hands or a spoon to mix the ingredients until they are well combined.
3. Form Loaf:
   - Transfer the turkey and spinach mixture into the prepared loaf pan.
   - Use your hands to shape it into a loaf shape, smoothing the top.
4. Bake:
   - Place the loaf pan in the preheated oven.
   - Bake for 45-55 minutes, or until the meatloaf is cooked through and the top is golden brown.

- To check for doneness, insert a meat thermometer into the center of the meatloaf. It should register at least 165°F (75°C).
5. Optional Topping:
    - If desired, spread a thin layer of ketchup or barbecue sauce on top of the meatloaf during the last 10 minutes of baking.
6. Rest and Serve:
    - Once the meatloaf is done baking, remove it from the oven and let it rest in the loaf pan for a few minutes.
    - Carefully transfer the meatloaf to a cutting board and slice it into thick slices.
    - Serve the Turkey and Spinach Meatloaf slices warm, alongside your favorite sides such as mashed potatoes, steamed vegetables, or a green salad.
7. Enjoy!
    - Enjoy this flavorful and nutritious Turkey and Spinach Meatloaf as a comforting meal for lunch or dinner. leftovers can be stored in an airtight container in the refrigerator for up to 3 days.

Greek Yogurt Chicken Salad Wraps

Ingredients:

For the Greek Yogurt Chicken Salad:

- 2 cups cooked chicken breast, shredded or diced
- 1/2 cup plain Greek yogurt
- 1/4 cup diced red onion
- 1/4 cup diced cucumber
- 1/4 cup diced bell pepper (any color)
- 1/4 cup diced celery
- 1/4 cup chopped fresh parsley
- 1 tablespoon lemon juice
- 1 tablespoon Dijon mustard
- Salt and pepper to taste

For the Wraps:

- 4 large whole wheat or spinach tortillas
- 2 cups baby spinach leaves
- Optional additions: sliced tomatoes, sliced avocado, crumbled feta cheese

Instructions:

1. Prepare Greek Yogurt Chicken Salad:
    - In a large mixing bowl, combine the cooked chicken breast, plain Greek yogurt, diced red onion, diced cucumber, diced bell pepper, diced celery, chopped fresh parsley, lemon juice, Dijon mustard, salt, and pepper.
    - Stir until all ingredients are well combined and the chicken is evenly coated with the yogurt mixture. Adjust seasoning to taste if needed.
2. Assemble Wraps:
    - Lay out the tortillas on a clean work surface.
    - Divide the baby spinach leaves evenly among the tortillas, spreading them out in a line down the center of each tortilla.

- Spoon the Greek yogurt chicken salad mixture on top of the spinach leaves, dividing it equally among the tortillas.
- If desired, add optional additions such as sliced tomatoes, sliced avocado, or crumbled feta cheese on top of the chicken salad.

3. Wrap:
    - To wrap each tortilla, fold the bottom edge up over the filling, then fold in the sides, and roll tightly from bottom to top to form a wrap.
    - Secure the wraps with toothpicks if needed to hold them together.

4. Serve:
    - Serve the Greek Yogurt Chicken Salad Wraps immediately, or wrap them tightly in plastic wrap or aluminum foil for later enjoyment.
    - They can be served chilled or at room temperature.

5. Enjoy!
    - Enjoy these flavorful and nutritious Greek Yogurt Chicken Salad Wraps as a satisfying meal for lunch or dinner. They're perfect for on-the-go or as a quick and easy meal option!

Tuna Salad Stuffed Avocados

Ingredients:

- 2 ripe avocados
- 1 can (5 oz) tuna, drained
- 1/4 cup diced red onion
- 1/4 cup diced celery
- 1/4 cup diced cucumber
- 2 tablespoons chopped fresh parsley or cilantro
- 2 tablespoons mayonnaise or Greek yogurt
- 1 tablespoon lemon juice
- Salt and pepper to taste
- Optional: sliced cherry tomatoes, sliced radishes, chopped chives for garnish

Instructions:

1. Prepare Avocados:
    - Slice the avocados in half lengthwise and remove the pits. Scoop out a little extra avocado flesh from each half to create a larger cavity for the tuna salad.
2. Prepare Tuna Salad:
    - In a mixing bowl, combine the drained tuna, diced red onion, diced celery, diced cucumber, chopped fresh parsley or cilantro, mayonnaise or Greek yogurt, and lemon juice.
    - Season with salt and pepper to taste.
    - Mix until all ingredients are well combined.
3. Stuff Avocados:
    - Spoon the tuna salad mixture into the cavities of the avocado halves, dividing it evenly among them.
    - Press the tuna salad gently into the avocado halves, mounding it slightly on top.
4. Garnish:
    - If desired, garnish the stuffed avocados with sliced cherry tomatoes, sliced radishes, or chopped chives for extra flavor and color.
5. Serve:
    - Serve the Tuna Salad Stuffed Avocados immediately as a nutritious and satisfying meal option for lunch or dinner.

- Enjoy them as is or with a side salad for a complete meal.
6. Enjoy!
    - Enjoy these tasty Tuna Salad Stuffed Avocados as a simple and flavorful dish that's packed with protein, healthy fats, and nutrients. They're perfect for a quick and easy meal!

Quinoa and Black Bean Stuffed Zucchini Boats

Ingredients:

- 4 medium zucchini
- 1 cup cooked quinoa
- 1 can (15 oz) black beans, drained and rinsed
- 1 cup corn kernels (fresh, canned, or frozen)
- 1 red bell pepper, diced
- 1/2 cup diced red onion
- 2 cloves garlic, minced
- 1 teaspoon ground cumin
- 1 teaspoon chili powder
- 1/2 teaspoon smoked paprika
- Salt and pepper to taste
- 1 cup shredded cheese (such as cheddar or Monterey Jack), divided
- Fresh cilantro or parsley, chopped (for garnish)
- Optional toppings: salsa, avocado slices, sour cream, lime wedges

Instructions:

1. Preheat Oven:
    - Preheat your oven to 400°F (200°C). Lightly grease a baking dish large enough to fit the zucchini boats.
2. Prepare Zucchini Boats:
    - Cut the zucchini in half lengthwise. Use a spoon to scoop out the flesh from the center of each zucchini half, leaving about 1/4 inch of flesh around the edges to create "boats." Reserve the scooped-out flesh for later use.
    - Place the zucchini boats in the prepared baking dish and set aside.
3. Prepare Filling:
    - In a large skillet, heat olive oil over medium heat. Add diced red onion and minced garlic, and cook until softened and fragrant, about 2-3 minutes.
    - Add diced red bell pepper and cook for another 2-3 minutes until slightly softened.
    - Add cooked quinoa, black beans, corn kernels, reserved zucchini flesh, ground cumin, chili powder, smoked paprika, salt, and pepper to the skillet.

Stir well to combine and cook for an additional 2-3 minutes until heated through.
- Remove the skillet from heat and stir in half of the shredded cheese until melted and well combined.

4. Stuff Zucchini Boats:
   - Spoon the quinoa and black bean mixture evenly into the hollowed-out zucchini boats, pressing gently to pack the filling.
   - Sprinkle the remaining shredded cheese on top of each stuffed zucchini boat.

5. Bake:
   - Cover the baking dish with foil and bake in the preheated oven for 20-25 minutes, or until the zucchini is tender and the filling is heated through and bubbly.

6. Garnish and Serve:
   - Remove the foil from the baking dish and switch the oven to broil. Broil the stuffed zucchini boats for 2-3 minutes, or until the cheese is golden and bubbly.
   - Remove from the oven and garnish with chopped fresh cilantro or parsley.
   - Serve the Quinoa and Black Bean Stuffed Zucchini Boats hot, with optional toppings such as salsa, avocado slices, sour cream, or lime wedges on the side.

7. Enjoy!
   - Enjoy these delicious and nutritious Quinoa and Black Bean Stuffed Zucchini Boats as a wholesome meal for lunch or dinner. They're packed with protein, fiber, and flavor!

Egg White Breakfast Burritos with Salsa

Ingredients:

- 4 large egg whites
- 2 whole wheat or spinach tortillas (8-inch diameter)
- 1/2 cup diced bell peppers (any color)
- 1/4 cup diced onion
- 1/4 cup diced tomatoes
- 1/4 cup shredded cheddar cheese (or cheese of your choice)
- Salt and pepper to taste
- Olive oil or cooking spray
- Salsa for serving

Instructions:

1. Prepare the Egg Whites:
    - In a bowl, whisk the egg whites until frothy. Season with salt and pepper to taste.
2. Cook the Vegetables:
    - Heat a small skillet over medium heat. Add a small amount of olive oil or coat with cooking spray.
    - Add the diced bell peppers and onion to the skillet. Cook for 2-3 minutes, or until the vegetables are softened.
3. Add the Egg Whites:
    - Pour the whisked egg whites into the skillet with the cooked vegetables. Stir gently to combine.
    - Cook the egg whites, stirring occasionally, until they are fully cooked and no longer runny.
4. Assemble the Burritos:
    - Warm the tortillas in a separate skillet or in the microwave for a few seconds to make them pliable.
    - Divide the cooked egg whites evenly between the two tortillas, placing them in the center of each tortilla.
    - Sprinkle diced tomatoes and shredded cheese over the egg whites on each tortilla.
5. Roll the Burritos:

- Fold the sides of each tortilla over the filling, then roll them up tightly from the bottom to form burritos.
6. Serve:
    - Serve the Egg White Breakfast Burritos with salsa on the side for dipping or drizzling.
    - You can also serve them with additional toppings like avocado slices, sour cream, or hot sauce if desired.
7. Enjoy!
    - Enjoy these delicious and protein-packed Egg White Breakfast Burritos with Salsa as a nutritious start to your day! They're quick to make and perfect for a satisfying breakfast on the go.

Turkey and Vegetable Lettuce Wraps

Ingredients:

For the Turkey Filling:

- 1 lb ground turkey
- 1 tablespoon olive oil
- 1 small onion, finely chopped
- 2 cloves garlic, minced
- 1 bell pepper, diced
- 1 carrot, grated
- 1 zucchini, diced
- 1 cup mushrooms, chopped
- 2 tablespoons soy sauce
- 1 tablespoon hoisin sauce
- 1 teaspoon ground ginger
- Salt and pepper to taste
- 1/4 cup chopped green onions (optional, for garnish)

For Serving:

- Large lettuce leaves (such as iceberg, butter, or romaine)
- Sriracha sauce or chili garlic sauce (optional, for extra heat)
- Lime wedges (optional, for garnish)

Instructions:

1. Prepare the Turkey Filling:
    - Heat olive oil in a large skillet over medium-high heat.
    - Add the ground turkey to the skillet and cook until browned, breaking it up with a spoon as it cooks.
    - Add the chopped onion and minced garlic to the skillet and cook for 2-3 minutes, or until softened and fragrant.

- Stir in the diced bell pepper, grated carrot, diced zucchini, and chopped mushrooms. Cook for another 5-7 minutes, or until the vegetables are tender.
- Add soy sauce, hoisin sauce, ground ginger, salt, and pepper to the skillet. Stir well to combine and cook for an additional 2-3 minutes to allow the flavors to meld.
- Taste and adjust seasoning if needed. Remove the skillet from heat.

2. Assemble Lettuce Wraps:
    - Wash and dry the lettuce leaves, then pat them dry with paper towels.
    - Spoon a portion of the turkey and vegetable mixture onto each lettuce leaf.
    - If desired, drizzle some sriracha sauce or chili garlic sauce over the filling for extra heat.
    - Garnish with chopped green onions and a squeeze of lime juice, if desired.

3. Serve:
    - Serve the Turkey and Vegetable Lettuce Wraps immediately, with extra lime wedges on the side for squeezing.
    - Enjoy them as a light and healthy meal option for lunch or dinner!

4. Enjoy!
    - Enjoy these flavorful and nutritious Turkey and Vegetable Lettuce Wraps as a satisfying meal. They're perfect for a quick and easy weeknight dinner or a light lunch!

Baked Chicken Tenders with Honey Mustard Dip

Ingredients:

For the Chicken Tenders:

- 1 lb chicken breast tenders or boneless, skinless chicken breasts, cut into strips
- 1 cup breadcrumbs (regular or panko)
- 1/4 cup grated Parmesan cheese
- 1 teaspoon garlic powder
- 1 teaspoon paprika
- 1/2 teaspoon salt
- 1/4 teaspoon black pepper
- 2 eggs, beaten
- Cooking spray or olive oil

For the Honey Mustard Dip:

- 1/4 cup mayonnaise
- 2 tablespoons Dijon mustard
- 2 tablespoons honey
- 1 tablespoon lemon juice
- Salt and pepper to taste

Instructions:

1. Preheat Oven:
   Preheat your oven to 400°F (200°C). Line a baking sheet with parchment paper or aluminum foil, and lightly grease it with cooking spray or olive oil.
2. Prepare Chicken Tenders:
    - In a shallow dish, mix together breadcrumbs, grated Parmesan cheese, garlic powder, paprika, salt, and black pepper.
    - In another shallow dish, beat the eggs.
    - Dip each chicken tender into the beaten eggs, then dredge it in the breadcrumb mixture, pressing gently to adhere the breadcrumbs to the chicken.

- Place the coated chicken tenders on the prepared baking sheet in a single layer.
3. Bake Chicken Tenders:
    - Lightly spray the tops of the chicken tenders with cooking spray or drizzle with olive oil.
    - Bake in the preheated oven for 15-20 minutes, or until the chicken is cooked through and the coating is golden brown and crispy.
4. Prepare Honey Mustard Dip:
    - While the chicken tenders are baking, prepare the honey mustard dip. In a small bowl, whisk together mayonnaise, Dijon mustard, honey, lemon juice, salt, and pepper until smooth and well combined.
    - Taste and adjust seasoning according to your preference.
5. Serve:
    - Once the chicken tenders are cooked, remove them from the oven and let them cool slightly.
    - Serve the baked chicken tenders warm with the honey mustard dip on the side for dipping.
6. Enjoy!
    - Enjoy these delicious Baked Chicken Tenders with Honey Mustard Dip as a tasty and satisfying meal or snack option. They're perfect for parties, game days, or family dinners!

Veggie and Egg Scramble

Ingredients:

- 4 eggs
- 1/4 cup milk (optional)
- 1 tablespoon butter or olive oil
- 1/2 cup diced bell peppers (any color)
- 1/2 cup diced onion
- 1/2 cup diced tomatoes
- 1/2 cup chopped spinach or kale
- Salt and pepper to taste
- Optional toppings: grated cheese, chopped herbs, hot sauce

Instructions:

1. Prepare Vegetables:
    - Heat butter or olive oil in a large skillet over medium heat.
    - Add diced bell peppers and onions to the skillet. Cook for 2-3 minutes until they start to soften.
2. Add Tomatoes and Greens:
    - Add diced tomatoes and chopped spinach or kale to the skillet. Cook for another 2-3 minutes until the vegetables are tender and the spinach or kale has wilted.
3. Scramble Eggs:
    - While the vegetables are cooking, crack the eggs into a bowl. Add milk if desired (for creamier eggs) and whisk until well beaten.
    - Pour the beaten eggs over the cooked vegetables in the skillet.
4. Scramble Eggs:
    - Using a spatula, gently scramble the eggs and vegetables together in the skillet. Continue to cook, stirring occasionally, until the eggs are cooked to your desired level of doneness.
5. Season and Serve:
    - Season the Veggie and Egg Scramble with salt and pepper to taste.
    - If desired, sprinkle grated cheese over the top and let it melt slightly.
    - Serve the scramble hot, garnished with chopped herbs or a drizzle of hot sauce if desired.

6. Enjoy!
    - Enjoy this Veggie and Egg Scramble for a nutritious and satisfying breakfast or brunch. It's versatile, customizable, and packed with flavor and nutrients!

Seared Salmon with Roasted Vegetables

Ingredients:

For the Seared Salmon:

- 4 salmon fillets, skin-on or skinless
- Salt and pepper to taste
- 2 tablespoons olive oil
- 1 lemon, sliced (for garnish)

For the Roasted Vegetables:

- 2 cups mixed vegetables (such as bell peppers, zucchini, cherry tomatoes, broccoli, cauliflower, carrots), chopped into bite-sized pieces
- 2 tablespoons olive oil
- 2 cloves garlic, minced
- 1 teaspoon dried herbs (such as thyme, rosemary, or Italian seasoning)
- Salt and pepper to taste

Instructions:

1. Preheat Oven:
   Preheat your oven to 400°F (200°C).
2. Prepare Salmon:
   - Pat the salmon fillets dry with paper towels and season both sides with salt and pepper.
   - Heat 2 tablespoons of olive oil in a large oven-safe skillet over medium-high heat.
   - Once the oil is hot, add the salmon fillets to the skillet, skin-side down if applicable.
   - Sear the salmon for 3-4 minutes on each side, until golden brown and crispy on the outside and cooked to your desired level of doneness. If using skin-on salmon, start with the skin-side down to get it crispy, then flip.
   - Remove the skillet from the heat. If desired, squeeze fresh lemon juice over the salmon fillets for added flavor.
3. Prepare Roasted Vegetables:

- In a large mixing bowl, toss the chopped mixed vegetables with 2 tablespoons of olive oil, minced garlic, dried herbs, salt, and pepper until evenly coated.
- Spread the seasoned vegetables in a single layer on a baking sheet lined with parchment paper or aluminum foil.

4. Roast Vegetables:
   - Roast the vegetables in the preheated oven for 20-25 minutes, or until tender and lightly browned, stirring halfway through cooking.
5. Serve:
   - Once the salmon is cooked and the vegetables are roasted, remove them from the oven.
   - Serve the seared salmon fillets hot, alongside the roasted vegetables.
   - Garnish with lemon slices for extra flavor and freshness.
6. Enjoy!
   - Enjoy this delicious and nutritious Seared Salmon with Roasted Vegetables as a wholesome and satisfying meal for lunch or dinner. It's packed with protein, healthy fats, and plenty of vitamins and minerals from the colorful vegetables!

Greek Yogurt Chicken Parmesan

Ingredients:

For the Chicken:

- 4 boneless, skinless chicken breasts
- Salt and pepper to taste
- 1 cup plain Greek yogurt
- 1 cup whole wheat breadcrumbs
- 1/2 cup grated Parmesan cheese
- 1 teaspoon garlic powder
- 1 teaspoon dried basil
- 1 teaspoon dried oregano
- Olive oil cooking spray

For the Sauce:

- 2 cups marinara sauce (store-bought or homemade)
- 1/2 teaspoon dried basil
- 1/2 teaspoon dried oregano
- 1/4 teaspoon red pepper flakes (optional)

For Topping:

- 1 cup shredded mozzarella cheese
- Fresh basil leaves, chopped (for garnish)

Instructions:

1. Preheat Oven:
   Preheat your oven to 400°F (200°C). Line a baking sheet with parchment paper or aluminum foil and set aside.
2. Prepare Chicken:

- Season both sides of the chicken breasts with salt and pepper.
- In a shallow dish, mix together Greek yogurt, garlic powder, dried basil, and dried oregano.
- In another shallow dish, combine breadcrumbs and grated Parmesan cheese.
- Dip each chicken breast into the Greek yogurt mixture, coating both sides evenly.
- Then dredge each chicken breast in the breadcrumb mixture, pressing gently to adhere the breadcrumbs.

3. Bake Chicken:
    - Place the coated chicken breasts on the prepared baking sheet.
    - Lightly spray the top of each chicken breast with olive oil cooking spray.
    - Bake in the preheated oven for 20-25 minutes, or until the chicken is cooked through and the coating is golden and crispy.
4. Prepare Sauce:
    - While the chicken is baking, heat marinara sauce in a small saucepan over medium heat.
    - Stir in dried basil, dried oregano, and red pepper flakes (if using). Simmer for 5-10 minutes to allow the flavors to meld.
5. Assemble Chicken Parmesan:
    - Once the chicken is cooked, remove it from the oven.
    - Spoon a generous amount of marinara sauce over each chicken breast.
    - Sprinkle shredded mozzarella cheese over the top of each chicken breast.
6. Finish Baking:
    - Return the chicken to the oven and bake for an additional 5-7 minutes, or until the cheese is melted and bubbly.
7. Serve:
    - Garnish the Chicken Parmesan with fresh chopped basil leaves.
    - Serve hot, accompanied by pasta, salad, or your favorite side dish.
8. Enjoy!
    - Enjoy this healthier version of Chicken Parmesan, made with Greek yogurt for added protein and flavor. It's a delicious and satisfying meal the whole family will love!

Shrimp and Avocado Lettuce Wraps

Ingredients:

For the Shrimp:

- 1 lb large shrimp, peeled and deveined
- 1 tablespoon olive oil
- 2 cloves garlic, minced
- 1 teaspoon paprika
- 1/2 teaspoon cumin
- Salt and pepper to taste
- Juice of 1 lime

For the Lettuce Wraps:

- Large lettuce leaves (such as butter lettuce or romaine)
- 2 avocados, sliced
- 1 cup cherry tomatoes, halved
- 1/4 cup red onion, thinly sliced
- Fresh cilantro leaves, chopped (for garnish)
- Lime wedges (for serving)

Instructions:

1. Prepare Shrimp:
    - In a large bowl, combine shrimp with olive oil, minced garlic, paprika, cumin, salt, pepper, and lime juice. Toss until the shrimp are evenly coated with the marinade.
2. Cook Shrimp:
    - Heat a large skillet over medium-high heat. Add the marinated shrimp to the skillet in a single layer.
    - Cook the shrimp for 2-3 minutes on each side, or until they are pink and opaque. Be careful not to overcook the shrimp, as they can become tough.
3. Assemble Lettuce Wraps:
    - Arrange the large lettuce leaves on a serving platter.
    - Place a few slices of avocado on each lettuce leaf.
    - Top with cooked shrimp, cherry tomatoes, and thinly sliced red onion.

4. Garnish and Serve:
    - Garnish the Shrimp and Avocado Lettuce Wraps with chopped fresh cilantro leaves.
    - Serve with lime wedges on the side for squeezing over the wraps.
5. Enjoy!
    - Enjoy these delicious and nutritious Shrimp and Avocado Lettuce Wraps as a light and refreshing meal or appetizer. They're perfect for a quick and easy lunch or dinner option!

Turkey and Sweet Potato Hash

Ingredients:

- 1 lb ground turkey
- 2 medium sweet potatoes, peeled and diced into small cubes
- 1 small onion, diced
- 2 cloves garlic, minced
- 1 bell pepper, diced
- 1 teaspoon ground cumin
- 1 teaspoon smoked paprika
- 1/2 teaspoon chili powder (optional)
- Salt and pepper to taste
- 2 tablespoons olive oil
- Fresh parsley or cilantro, chopped (for garnish)
- Fried or poached eggs (optional, for serving)

Instructions:

1. Cook Sweet Potatoes:
    - Heat 1 tablespoon of olive oil in a large skillet over medium heat. Add the diced sweet potatoes to the skillet and cook, stirring occasionally, until they are tender and lightly browned, about 8-10 minutes. Remove the sweet potatoes from the skillet and set aside.
2. Cook Turkey:
    - In the same skillet, heat the remaining tablespoon of olive oil over medium heat. Add the diced onion and bell pepper to the skillet and cook until softened, about 3-4 minutes.
    - Add the ground turkey to the skillet, breaking it up with a spoon. Cook until the turkey is browned and cooked through, about 5-6 minutes.
3. Combine Ingredients:
    - Return the cooked sweet potatoes to the skillet with the turkey mixture. Add minced garlic, ground cumin, smoked paprika, chili powder (if using), salt, and pepper. Stir well to combine all the ingredients.
4. Finish Cooking:

- Cook the hash for an additional 3-4 minutes, stirring occasionally, until everything is heated through and well combined. Adjust seasoning to taste if needed.

5. Serve:
    - Serve the Turkey and Sweet Potato Hash hot, garnished with chopped fresh parsley or cilantro.
    - Optionally, serve with fried or poached eggs on top for added protein and richness.
6. Enjoy!
    - Enjoy this hearty and flavorful Turkey and Sweet Potato Hash as a delicious and satisfying breakfast, brunch, or dinner option!

Grilled Vegetable Quinoa Bowl

Ingredients:

For the Quinoa:

- 1 cup quinoa
- 2 cups water or vegetable broth
- Salt to taste

For the Grilled Vegetables:

- 2 cups mixed vegetables (such as bell peppers, zucchini, eggplant, cherry tomatoes, red onion)
- 2 tablespoons olive oil
- 2 cloves garlic, minced
- 1 teaspoon dried herbs (such as thyme, rosemary, or Italian seasoning)
- Salt and pepper to taste

For the Lemon Herb Dressing:

- 1/4 cup olive oil
- 2 tablespoons lemon juice
- 1 tablespoon fresh parsley, chopped
- 1 tablespoon fresh basil, chopped
- 1 clove garlic, minced
- Salt and pepper to taste

Optional Toppings:

- Crumbled feta cheese
- Toasted pine nuts or almonds
- Avocado slices
- Fresh herbs for garnish

Instructions:

1. Prepare Quinoa:
   - Rinse the quinoa under cold water in a fine-mesh strainer to remove any bitterness.
   - In a saucepan, combine the quinoa and water or vegetable broth. Bring to a boil, then reduce the heat to low, cover, and simmer for 15-20 minutes, or until the quinoa is cooked and the liquid is absorbed. Fluff the quinoa with a fork and season with salt to taste. Set aside.
2. Prepare Grilled Vegetables:
   - Preheat your grill or grill pan over medium-high heat.
   - In a large bowl, toss the mixed vegetables with olive oil, minced garlic, dried herbs, salt, and pepper until evenly coated.
   - Grill the vegetables for 5-7 minutes per side, or until tender and lightly charred. Remove from the grill and set aside.
3. Prepare Lemon Herb Dressing:
   - In a small bowl, whisk together olive oil, lemon juice, chopped parsley, chopped basil, minced garlic, salt, and pepper until well combined. Set aside.
4. Assemble Quinoa Bowls:
   - Divide the cooked quinoa evenly among serving bowls.
   - Top each bowl with grilled vegetables.
   - Drizzle the lemon herb dressing over the quinoa and vegetables.
5. Add Optional Toppings:
   - If desired, sprinkle crumbled feta cheese and toasted pine nuts or almonds over the quinoa bowls.
   - Add avocado slices for extra creaminess.
6. Garnish and Serve:
   - Garnish the Grilled Vegetable Quinoa Bowls with fresh herbs for a pop of color and freshness.
   - Serve immediately and enjoy!
7. Enjoy!
   - Enjoy these flavorful and nutritious Grilled Vegetable Quinoa Bowls as a wholesome and satisfying meal for lunch or dinner!

Baked Chicken Drumsticks with Roasted Cauliflower

Ingredients:

For the Baked Chicken Drumsticks:

- 8 chicken drumsticks
- 2 tablespoons olive oil
- 2 cloves garlic, minced
- 1 teaspoon paprika
- 1 teaspoon dried thyme
- 1 teaspoon dried oregano
- Salt and pepper to taste

For the Roasted Cauliflower:

- 1 large head cauliflower, cut into florets
- 2 tablespoons olive oil
- 1 teaspoon garlic powder
- 1 teaspoon paprika
- Salt and pepper to taste

Instructions:

1. Preheat Oven:
   Preheat your oven to 425°F (220°C). Line a baking sheet with parchment paper or aluminum foil and set aside.
2. Prepare Chicken Drumsticks:
   - In a large bowl, combine olive oil, minced garlic, paprika, dried thyme, dried oregano, salt, and pepper.
   - Add the chicken drumsticks to the bowl and toss until they are evenly coated with the marinade.
3. Bake Chicken Drumsticks:
   - Place the marinated chicken drumsticks on the prepared baking sheet, spacing them apart.

- Bake in the preheated oven for 35-40 minutes, or until the chicken is golden brown and cooked through, with an internal temperature of 165°F (75°C).
4. Prepare Roasted Cauliflower:
    - While the chicken is baking, prepare the roasted cauliflower.
    - In a large bowl, toss the cauliflower florets with olive oil, garlic powder, paprika, salt, and pepper until evenly coated.
5. Roast Cauliflower:
    - Spread the seasoned cauliflower florets in a single layer on a separate baking sheet.
    - Place the baking sheet in the oven alongside the chicken drumsticks and roast for 25-30 minutes, or until the cauliflower is tender and golden brown, stirring halfway through cooking.
6. Serve:
    - Once the chicken drumsticks and roasted cauliflower are cooked, remove them from the oven.
    - Serve the baked chicken drumsticks and roasted cauliflower hot as a delicious and nutritious meal.
7. Enjoy!
    - Enjoy this flavorful and satisfying Baked Chicken Drumsticks with Roasted Cauliflower for a wholesome dinner option that's sure to please the whole family!

Mediterranean Chickpea Salad with Feta

Ingredients:

For the Salad:

- 2 cans (15 ounces each) chickpeas (garbanzo beans), drained and rinsed
- 1 cucumber, diced
- 1 cup cherry tomatoes, halved
- 1/2 red onion, thinly sliced
- 1/2 cup Kalamata olives, pitted and sliced
- 1/2 cup crumbled feta cheese
- 1/4 cup fresh parsley, chopped
- 1/4 cup fresh mint leaves, chopped (optional)

For the Dressing:

- 1/4 cup extra virgin olive oil
- 2 tablespoons red wine vinegar
- 1 clove garlic, minced
- 1 teaspoon dried oregano
- Salt and pepper to taste

Instructions:

1. Prepare Chickpeas:
   - Rinse the canned chickpeas under cold water in a colander to remove excess salt and drain well. Transfer them to a large mixing bowl.
2. Assemble Salad:
   - To the bowl with chickpeas, add diced cucumber, halved cherry tomatoes, thinly sliced red onion, sliced Kalamata olives, crumbled feta cheese, chopped parsley, and chopped mint leaves (if using). Toss gently to combine.
3. Prepare Dressing:
   - In a small bowl, whisk together extra virgin olive oil, red wine vinegar, minced garlic, dried oregano, salt, and pepper until well combined.

4. Dress Salad:
    - Pour the dressing over the chickpea salad and toss until all ingredients are evenly coated with the dressing.
5. Chill:
    - Cover the salad with plastic wrap or transfer it to an airtight container. Refrigerate for at least 30 minutes to allow the flavors to meld and develop.
6. Serve:
    - Once chilled, give the salad a final toss and adjust seasoning if needed.
    - Serve the Mediterranean Chickpea Salad with Feta as a refreshing side dish or light main course.
7. Enjoy!
    - Enjoy the fresh and vibrant flavors of this Mediterranean-inspired salad, perfect for picnics, potlucks, or as a healthy meal option any day of the week!

Egg White Breakfast Muffins with Spinach and Feta

Ingredients:

- 2 cups egg whites (from about 8 large eggs)
- 1 cup fresh spinach, chopped
- 1/2 cup crumbled feta cheese
- 1/4 cup diced red bell pepper
- 1/4 cup diced red onion
- 2 cloves garlic, minced
- Salt and pepper to taste
- Cooking spray or olive oil, for greasing muffin tin

Instructions:

1. Preheat Oven:
   Preheat your oven to 350°F (175°C). Grease a 12-cup muffin tin with cooking spray or olive oil and set aside.
2. Prepare Ingredients:
   - In a mixing bowl, whisk together the egg whites until slightly frothy.
   - Add chopped spinach, crumbled feta cheese, diced red bell pepper, diced red onion, minced garlic, salt, and pepper to the bowl. Stir until all ingredients are well combined.
3. Fill Muffin Cups:
   - Pour the egg white mixture evenly into the prepared muffin cups, filling each cup about 2/3 full.
4. Bake:
   - Place the muffin tin in the preheated oven and bake for 20-25 minutes, or until the egg white muffins are set and lightly golden on top.
5. Cool and Serve:
   - Remove the muffin tin from the oven and let the egg white muffins cool in the tin for a few minutes.
   - Use a butter knife to gently loosen the edges of the muffins, then carefully remove them from the tin and transfer to a wire rack to cool completely.
6. Enjoy!
   - Once cooled, these Egg White Breakfast Muffins with Spinach and Feta are ready to be enjoyed! They make a delicious and nutritious breakfast or

snack option that's packed with protein and flavor. Store any leftovers in an airtight container in the refrigerator for up to 3-4 days. Enjoy!

Turkey and Vegetable Kabobs with Quinoa

Ingredients:

For the Turkey and Vegetable Kabobs:

- 1 lb turkey breast or turkey tenderloin, cut into cubes
- 2 bell peppers (any color), cut into chunks
- 1 large red onion, cut into chunks
- 1 zucchini, sliced into rounds
- 8-10 cherry tomatoes
- Wooden or metal skewers

For the Marinade:

- 1/4 cup olive oil
- 2 tablespoons soy sauce or tamari
- 2 cloves garlic, minced
- 1 teaspoon dried oregano
- 1 teaspoon dried thyme
- Salt and pepper to taste

For the Quinoa:

- 1 cup quinoa
- 2 cups water or vegetable broth
- Salt to taste

For Serving:

- Fresh parsley or cilantro, chopped (for garnish)
- Lemon wedges (for serving)

Instructions:

1. Marinate the Turkey:

- In a bowl, whisk together the olive oil, soy sauce or tamari, minced garlic, dried oregano, dried thyme, salt, and pepper to make the marinade.
- Place the cubed turkey in a shallow dish or a large resealable plastic bag. Pour the marinade over the turkey, making sure it's evenly coated. Cover or seal and refrigerate for at least 30 minutes, or up to 2 hours.

2. Prepare the Quinoa:
    - Rinse the quinoa under cold water in a fine-mesh strainer to remove any bitterness.
    - In a saucepan, combine the quinoa and water or vegetable broth. Bring to a boil, then reduce the heat to low, cover, and simmer for 15-20 minutes, or until the quinoa is cooked and the liquid is absorbed. Fluff the quinoa with a fork and season with salt to taste. Set aside.

3. Assemble the Kabobs:
    - Preheat your grill or grill pan over medium-high heat.
    - Thread the marinated turkey cubes, bell pepper chunks, red onion chunks, zucchini slices, and cherry tomatoes onto the skewers, alternating the ingredients as desired.

4. Grill the Kabobs:
    - Lightly oil the grill grates or grill pan to prevent sticking.
    - Place the assembled kabobs on the preheated grill and cook for 8-10 minutes, turning occasionally, or until the turkey is cooked through and the vegetables are tender and lightly charred.

5. Serve:
    - Divide the cooked quinoa among serving plates or bowls.
    - Remove the turkey and vegetable kabobs from the grill and carefully slide the cooked ingredients off the skewers onto the quinoa.
    - Garnish with chopped fresh parsley or cilantro and serve with lemon wedges on the side for squeezing over the kabobs.

6. Enjoy!
    - Enjoy these flavorful Turkey and Vegetable Kabobs with Quinoa as a healthy and satisfying meal! They're perfect for summer grilling or any time of the year.

Baked Cod with Tomato and Olive Relish

Ingredients:

For the Baked Cod:

- 4 cod fillets (about 6 ounces each)
- 2 tablespoons olive oil
- 2 cloves garlic, minced
- 1 teaspoon paprika
- 1 teaspoon dried oregano
- Salt and pepper to taste
- Lemon wedges for serving

For the Tomato and Olive Relish:

- 1 cup cherry tomatoes, halved
- 1/4 cup Kalamata olives, pitted and chopped
- 2 tablespoons capers, drained
- 2 tablespoons fresh parsley, chopped
- 1 tablespoon extra virgin olive oil
- 1 tablespoon lemon juice
- Salt and pepper to taste

Instructions:

1. Preheat Oven:
   Preheat your oven to 400°F (200°C). Grease a baking dish with olive oil or line it with parchment paper.
2. Prepare the Cod:
   - Pat the cod fillets dry with paper towels and place them in the prepared baking dish.
   - In a small bowl, whisk together the olive oil, minced garlic, paprika, dried oregano, salt, and pepper. Brush the mixture over the cod fillets, coating them evenly.
3. Bake the Cod:

- Place the baking dish in the preheated oven and bake for 12-15 minutes, or until the cod is opaque and flakes easily with a fork.
4. Make the Tomato and Olive Relish:
    - In a mixing bowl, combine the halved cherry tomatoes, chopped Kalamata olives, drained capers, chopped fresh parsley, extra virgin olive oil, lemon juice, salt, and pepper. Toss until all the ingredients are well combined.
5. Serve:
    - Once the cod is baked, remove it from the oven and let it rest for a few minutes.
    - Spoon the tomato and olive relish over the baked cod fillets.
    - Serve the Baked Cod with Tomato and Olive Relish hot, garnished with additional fresh parsley and lemon wedges on the side.
6. Enjoy!
    - Enjoy this flavorful and healthy Baked Cod with Tomato and Olive Relish as a delicious main course. It's perfect for a light and satisfying dinner!

Chicken and Quinoa Power Bowl

Ingredients:

For the Chicken:

- 2 boneless, skinless chicken breasts
- 2 tablespoons olive oil
- 1 teaspoon paprika
- 1 teaspoon garlic powder
- 1 teaspoon dried thyme
- Salt and pepper to taste

For the Quinoa:

- 1 cup quinoa
- 2 cups water or chicken broth
- Salt to taste

For the Power Bowl:

- 2 cups mixed greens (such as spinach, kale, or arugula)
- 1 cup cherry tomatoes, halved
- 1 cucumber, diced
- 1 avocado, sliced
- 1/4 cup red onion, thinly sliced
- 1/4 cup crumbled feta cheese (optional)
- Lemon wedges for serving

For the Dressing:

- 1/4 cup olive oil
- 2 tablespoons lemon juice
- 1 tablespoon Dijon mustard
- 1 clove garlic, minced
- Salt and pepper to taste

Instructions:

1. Prepare the Chicken:
    - In a small bowl, mix together olive oil, paprika, garlic powder, dried thyme, salt, and pepper to create a marinade.
    - Place the chicken breasts in a shallow dish and pour the marinade over them, making sure they are evenly coated. Let them marinate for at least 30 minutes, or refrigerate overnight for best results.
2. Cook the Quinoa:
    - Rinse the quinoa under cold water in a fine-mesh strainer to remove any bitterness.
    - In a saucepan, combine the quinoa and water or chicken broth. Bring to a boil, then reduce the heat to low, cover, and simmer for 15-20 minutes, or until the quinoa is cooked and the liquid is absorbed. Fluff the quinoa with a fork and season with salt to taste. Set aside.
3. Cook the Chicken:
    - Heat a grill pan or skillet over medium-high heat. Remove the chicken breasts from the marinade and discard any excess marinade.
    - Cook the chicken breasts for 6-8 minutes per side, or until they are cooked through and reach an internal temperature of 165°F (75°C). Remove from heat and let them rest for a few minutes before slicing.
4. Assemble the Power Bowl:
    - Divide the mixed greens among serving bowls. Top with cooked quinoa, cherry tomatoes, diced cucumber, sliced avocado, thinly sliced red onion, and sliced chicken breasts.
5. Make the Dressing:
    - In a small bowl, whisk together olive oil, lemon juice, Dijon mustard, minced garlic, salt, and pepper until well combined.
6. Drizzle the Dressing:
    - Drizzle the dressing over the assembled power bowls.
7. Optional Toppings:
    - If desired, sprinkle crumbled feta cheese over the power bowls for extra flavor.
8. Serve:
    - Serve the Chicken and Quinoa Power Bowls with lemon wedges on the side for squeezing over the bowls.
9. Enjoy!

- Enjoy this nutritious and flavorful Chicken and Quinoa Power Bowl as a wholesome meal that's packed with protein, fiber, and essential nutrients!

Turkey and Vegetable Stir-Fry with Brown Rice

Ingredients:

For the Stir-Fry:

- 1 lb ground turkey
- 2 tablespoons vegetable oil
- 2 cloves garlic, minced
- 1 tablespoon ginger, minced
- 1 onion, thinly sliced
- 2 bell peppers, thinly sliced (any color)
- 2 cups broccoli florets
- 1 cup snap peas
- Salt and pepper to taste
- Sesame seeds for garnish (optional)
- Sliced green onions for garnish (optional)

For the Stir-Fry Sauce:

- 1/4 cup soy sauce
- 2 tablespoons hoisin sauce
- 1 tablespoon rice vinegar
- 1 tablespoon honey or brown sugar
- 1 teaspoon sesame oil
- 1 teaspoon cornstarch (optional, for thickening)

For the Brown Rice:

- 1 cup brown rice
- 2 cups water
- Salt to taste

Instructions:

1. Prepare the Brown Rice:
    - Rinse the brown rice under cold water until the water runs clear.

- In a saucepan, combine the brown rice, water, and salt. Bring to a boil over high heat.
- Reduce the heat to low, cover, and simmer for 40-45 minutes, or until the rice is tender and the water is absorbed. Remove from heat and let it sit covered for 5 minutes. Fluff with a fork and set aside.

2. Prepare the Stir-Fry Sauce:
   - In a small bowl, whisk together the soy sauce, hoisin sauce, rice vinegar, honey or brown sugar, sesame oil, and cornstarch (if using). Set aside.
3. Cook the Ground Turkey:
   - Heat one tablespoon of vegetable oil in a large skillet or wok over medium-high heat.
   - Add the ground turkey to the skillet and cook, breaking it up with a spoon, until it is browned and cooked through. Remove the cooked turkey from the skillet and set aside.
4. Cook the Vegetables:
   - In the same skillet, heat the remaining tablespoon of vegetable oil over medium-high heat.
   - Add the minced garlic and ginger to the skillet and cook for 1-2 minutes, until fragrant.
   - Add the thinly sliced onion, bell peppers, broccoli florets, and snap peas to the skillet. Stir-fry for 5-6 minutes, or until the vegetables are tender-crisp.
5. Combine Turkey and Vegetables:
   - Return the cooked ground turkey to the skillet with the cooked vegetables. Stir to combine.
6. Add Stir-Fry Sauce:
   - Pour the prepared stir-fry sauce over the turkey and vegetables in the skillet. Stir well to coat everything evenly.
   - Cook for another 2-3 minutes, or until the sauce has thickened slightly.
7. Serve:
   - Serve the Turkey and Vegetable Stir-Fry over cooked brown rice.
   - Garnish with sesame seeds and sliced green onions, if desired.
8. Enjoy!
   - Enjoy this delicious and nutritious Turkey and Vegetable Stir-Fry with Brown Rice as a satisfying meal for lunch or dinner!

Grilled Chicken Caesar Salad

Ingredients:

For the Grilled Chicken:

- 2 boneless, skinless chicken breasts
- 2 tablespoons olive oil
- 2 cloves garlic, minced
- 1 teaspoon dried oregano
- 1 teaspoon dried thyme
- Salt and pepper to taste

For the Caesar Salad:

- 1 large head of romaine lettuce, washed and chopped
- 1/2 cup croutons
- 1/4 cup grated Parmesan cheese
- Caesar dressing (homemade or store-bought)

Instructions:

1. Marinate the Chicken:
    - In a bowl, combine olive oil, minced garlic, dried oregano, dried thyme, salt, and pepper.
    - Place the chicken breasts in the marinade, turning to coat evenly. Cover and refrigerate for at least 30 minutes, or up to 4 hours.
2. Preheat the Grill:
    - Preheat your grill to medium-high heat.
3. Grill the Chicken:
    - Remove the chicken breasts from the marinade and discard any excess marinade.
    - Grill the chicken breasts for 6-8 minutes per side, or until they are cooked through and no longer pink in the center. The internal temperature should reach 165°F (75°C).

- Once cooked, transfer the chicken to a cutting board and let it rest for a few minutes before slicing.
4. Prepare the Salad:
    - In a large salad bowl, combine the chopped romaine lettuce, croutons, and grated Parmesan cheese.
5. Assemble the Salad:
    - Slice the grilled chicken breasts into thin strips.
    - Add the sliced chicken to the salad bowl with the romaine lettuce, croutons, and Parmesan cheese.
    - Drizzle Caesar dressing over the salad, tossing gently to coat everything evenly.
6. Serve:
    - Divide the Grilled Chicken Caesar Salad among serving plates or bowls.
    - Garnish with additional grated Parmesan cheese and freshly ground black pepper, if desired.
7. Enjoy!
    - Enjoy this classic Grilled Chicken Caesar Salad as a delicious and satisfying meal for lunch or dinner! It's packed with flavor and perfect for summer grilling or any time of the year.

Veggie-Packed Egg White Frittata

Ingredients:

- 8 large egg whites
- 2 whole eggs
- 1/4 cup milk (or non-dairy milk)
- 1 tablespoon olive oil
- 1 small onion, diced
- 1 bell pepper, diced
- 1 cup chopped spinach
- 1 cup sliced mushrooms
- 1 tomato, diced
- Salt and pepper to taste
- 1/4 cup grated cheese (optional, for topping)
- Fresh herbs for garnish (optional)

Instructions:

1. Preheat the Oven:
   Preheat your oven to 375°F (190°C).
2. Prepare the Vegetables:
   - In a large oven-safe skillet, heat olive oil over medium heat.
   - Add diced onion and cook until translucent, about 3-4 minutes.
   - Add diced bell pepper and sliced mushrooms, and cook for another 3-4 minutes until the vegetables are softened.
   - Stir in chopped spinach and diced tomato, and cook for an additional 1-2 minutes until the spinach wilts. Season with salt and pepper to taste.
3. Prepare the Egg Mixture:
   - In a mixing bowl, whisk together the egg whites, whole eggs, and milk until well combined.
4. Assemble the Frittata:
   - Pour the egg mixture over the cooked vegetables in the skillet, ensuring the eggs are evenly distributed.
   - Use a spatula to gently stir the mixture, allowing the vegetables to evenly distribute throughout the eggs.
5. Bake the Frittata:

- Transfer the skillet to the preheated oven and bake for 15-20 minutes, or until the frittata is set in the center and lightly golden on top.
6. Add Toppings (Optional):
    - If desired, sprinkle grated cheese over the top of the frittata during the last few minutes of baking until melted and bubbly.
7. Serve:
    - Once baked, remove the frittata from the oven and let it cool slightly in the skillet.
    - Slice the frittata into wedges or squares and garnish with fresh herbs, if using.
8. Enjoy!
    - Serve the Veggie-Packed Egg White Frittata warm or at room temperature for a nutritious and delicious breakfast, brunch, or light dinner option. It's packed with protein and loaded with veggies for a healthy meal!

Lentil and Chickpea Salad with Lemon Vinaigrette

Ingredients:

For the Salad:

- 1 cup green lentils, rinsed
- 1 can (15 oz) chickpeas, drained and rinsed
- 1 cup cherry tomatoes, halved
- 1 cucumber, diced
- 1/4 cup red onion, finely chopped
- 1/4 cup fresh parsley, chopped
- 1/4 cup fresh cilantro, chopped (optional)
- Salt and black pepper to taste

For the Lemon Vinaigrette:

- 1/4 cup extra virgin olive oil
- Zest and juice of 1 lemon
- 2 cloves garlic, minced
- 1 teaspoon Dijon mustard
- 1 teaspoon honey or maple syrup
- Salt and black pepper to taste

Instructions:

1. Cook the Lentils:
    - In a medium saucepan, combine the rinsed lentils with 2 cups of water. Bring to a boil over medium-high heat.
    - Reduce the heat to low, cover, and simmer for 20-25 minutes, or until the lentils are tender but still hold their shape. Drain any excess water and set aside to cool.
2. Prepare the Vinaigrette:
    - In a small bowl, whisk together the olive oil, lemon zest, lemon juice, minced garlic, Dijon mustard, honey or maple syrup, salt, and black pepper until well combined. Set aside.
3. Assemble the Salad:

- In a large salad bowl, combine the cooked lentils, chickpeas, halved cherry tomatoes, diced cucumber, finely chopped red onion, chopped parsley, and cilantro (if using).
- Season the salad with salt and black pepper to taste.
4. Dress the Salad:
    - Pour the prepared lemon vinaigrette over the salad and toss gently to coat all the ingredients evenly.
5. Chill and Serve:
    - Cover the salad bowl with plastic wrap or transfer the salad to an airtight container. Refrigerate for at least 30 minutes to allow the flavors to meld together.
    - Serve the Lentil and Chickpea Salad chilled as a refreshing and nutritious meal or side dish.
6. Enjoy!
    - Enjoy the vibrant flavors and textures of this Lentil and Chickpea Salad with Lemon Vinaigrette. It's packed with protein, fiber, and fresh ingredients, making it a perfect option for a light and satisfying meal!

Quinoa and Black Bean Veggie Burgers

Ingredients:

- 1 cup cooked quinoa
- 1 can (15 oz) black beans, drained and rinsed
- 1/2 cup rolled oats (or breadcrumbs)
- 1/2 cup finely chopped onion
- 1/2 cup grated carrot
- 1/4 cup chopped fresh cilantro
- 2 cloves garlic, minced
- 1 teaspoon ground cumin
- 1 teaspoon chili powder
- 1/2 teaspoon smoked paprika
- Salt and pepper to taste
- 1 tablespoon olive oil (for cooking)

Optional Toppings:

- Whole grain burger buns
- Lettuce leaves
- Sliced tomatoes
- Sliced avocado
- Red onion slices
- Mustard or ketchup

Instructions:

1. Prepare the Quinoa and Black Beans:
    - Cook the quinoa according to package instructions and allow it to cool.
    - In a large mixing bowl, mash the black beans with a fork or potato masher until mostly smooth but still slightly chunky.
2. Mix the Burger Ingredients:
    - To the mashed black beans, add the cooked quinoa, rolled oats (or breadcrumbs), finely chopped onion, grated carrot, chopped cilantro, minced garlic, ground cumin, chili powder, smoked paprika, salt, and pepper. Mix until well combined.
3. Form the Patties:

- Divide the mixture into 4-6 equal portions, depending on the desired size of your burgers. Shape each portion into a patty, compacting them slightly with your hands to ensure they hold together.

4. Cook the Patties:
   - Heat the olive oil in a skillet over medium heat. Once hot, add the burger patties to the skillet (you may need to cook them in batches).
   - Cook the patties for 4-5 minutes on each side, or until they are golden brown and crispy on the outside, and heated through.

5. Assemble the Burgers:
   - Toast the burger buns lightly if desired.
   - Place a lettuce leaf on the bottom half of each burger bun, followed by a quinoa and black bean patty.
   - Top the patties with sliced tomatoes, avocado slices, red onion slices, and any other desired toppings.
   - Spread mustard or ketchup on the top half of each burger bun, then place it on top of the assembled burger.

6. Serve and Enjoy!
   - Serve the Quinoa and Black Bean Veggie Burgers immediately, with your favorite side dishes or salad. Enjoy the delicious and nutritious plant-based meal!

www.ingramcontent.com/pod-product-compliance
Lightning Source LLC
LaVergne TN
LVHW081559060526
838201LV00054B/1979